preparing for
a career in

ART and DESIGN

Published by the
Association of Independent Colleges
of Art and Design

EDITOR

William O. Barrett
Executive Director, AICAD

CONTRIBUTING WRITER

Scott Mandell
San Francisco, CA

DESIGN

Melanie Doherty Design
San Francisco, CA

CONTENTS

INTRODUCTION

This book is intended as a resource primarily for high school students who are grappling with questions about careers and higher education in the visual arts. It will also be helpful to the parents, art teachers, and guidance counselors of these students. And older students contemplating entry into the fields of art and design should find relevant information here as well.

We will review the educational options available to prospective artists and designers, explain 30 different careers in the visual arts through profiles of successful practitioners, and provide other career and education resources. Because this book is aimed at students just entering the art and design fields, it includes only passing mention of the Master of Fine Arts and other graduate-level programs.

Pursuing a career can be both pleasurable and pressured. The pleasure is because a career can lead to a lifetime of satisfying work. The pressure is because careers are closely tied your own identity, perceptions, and skills. Embarking on a career can be one of life's biggest joys. However, the process of choosing is not made any easier by the existence of negative stereotypes about art careers (which this book attempts to refute through its career profiles). Our goal is to demystify this subject and thus remove some of the distress that naturally comes when beginning a career.

In the past decade, the anxiety surrounding the subject of college and career choices has risen to near frenzy levels. This seems to us entirely unnecessary, for there are more possibilities available to young students today than at any time in history. Perhaps our first piece of advice, then, is to relax! These may be big decisions, but the world will not end if you do not achieve absolute perfection in answering them by the time you graduate from high school. Keeping your mind open to change and to new ideas, and realizing that the only person you really have to satisfy is yourself, will help immeasurably. We hope this book will help as well.

ACKNOWLEDGEMENTS

The editor extends deep appreciation to all those who made this book possible. Key among them are the artists and designers who contributed their work and biographies, as well as the many staff members at AICAD colleges who facilitated the gathering of this material. Special thanks goes to the AICAD Board of Directors, especially its Communications Committee, for their support, advice and patience. Grateful thanks too for the able assistance of Diane Nesin, Diane Barrett, Jeff Henne, and David Brown.

4

Artists and designers are central to our culture and our commerce; indeed, our society would not be where it is today without them. Fine artists create their own expressive images that can please and educate us or shock and challenge us. Designers shape the things we use and live with every day, and their impact is growing steadily because so much of our new technology is visually based. Visual material is a basic and ubiquitous component of our everyday lives. Because of this, the fields of art and design offer countless opportunities for satisfying careers and meaningful lives.

CHAPTER 1

Preparing for Your Career

Photos by Todd Hido

Getting there is not quick or automatic, of course. The enjoyment of a career naturally requires some effort as well. There are skills, processes, and traditions to learn. There is endless work and practice to build a sufficient level of expertise. This takes time and effort, coupled with occasional sacrifice. Yet in the end, you come away with the satisfaction of knowing that you are creating things and affecting society as very few others can.

How do I know this is for me?

It is normal to wonder whether you can "make the grade" in art or design; certainty is hard to achieve when making such a complex decision as "what to do with your life." A good early sign of potential is if you spend a lot of time in visual activity such as sketching, taking photographs, making things with your hands, rearranging colors, or doing similar things. If you have taken art courses and received positive reviews of your work, this is an even stronger sign that you have the talent to succeed. More than anything else, your own motivation can be not only a major source of strength but an important sign you are doing the right thing. If you are continually attracted to art and design work, if it is something you feel compelled to do, then it is probably wise to heed those "signs."

If you are undecided about an art and design career, you might look for some additional experience to see if this brings more clarity. For instance, most art colleges and some large art departments offer summer courses specifically for high school students. Often these kinds of programs are available during the regular school year as well. If you cannot take a pre-college course or you remain undecided after you have, then it is perfectly acceptable to just make the best choice you can and see how you feel after you gain a more experience. Sometimes you can't project what something will be like until you actually do it. And changing colleges (transferring) is relatively common these days, and it is even more common to change careers throughout a lifetime. So, after relaxing, think it through, do the best you can, and then see what happens.

Is a college education required?

A simplistic answer is no. In art and design there are few disciplines with formal education requirements. Indeed, until shortly after World War II, going to college was unusual in most visual art fields. Artists and designers were often self-trained or educated through apprenticeships and on-the-job training. Many artists and designers working today are self-

taught, and future practitioners with outstanding energy and diligence are not prevented from entering most career areas in the same way. (For a discussion of the terms fine artist, craftsperson, and designer, please see the beginning of Chapter 2.)

However, the current complexity of our society and of the art and design fields, the expectations of employers and art venues, and the increasing competition from college-educated students for employment positions have all come together to create a situation in which going to college is becoming a necessity. The days of being an apprentice or learning on the job are largely past; college has assumed that role to a great extent. Graduating with a professional degree is already a requirement in architecture, and other design fields are expected to evolve that same way over time. In most design disciplines it is now quite common for employers to expect, or even require, a BFA degree from job applicants.

In fine arts and crafts areas there is less "official" pressure to attend college or have a degree, and people can still pursue these areas with little or no formal professional education. On the other hand, because of the steadily increasing number of artists with higher education experience, the fine arts have become competitive enough that college is, if not required, at least highly desirable. A quick review of catalogs from contemporary group art shows will reveal that most young artists have a BFA and/or an MFA. While virtually no art galleries, museums, or craft outlets require a degree, the experience of higher education offers a clear boost to students about to start their careers. And for those who want to teach at the K–12 or college level, undergraduate degrees are essential and graduate degrees are often required.

Can you make it without college? Yes you can, if you are among the rare group of people who are exceptionally gifted and diligent. But for most people in art, as in many other fields, college is where you learn and hone skills and creativity. It is now normal for most artists and designers to have a professional education.

College-level art and design programs have the advantage of providing a group of motivated, talented students and faculty to interact and "network" with (hard to do on your own), and of compressing countless years of self-study experiences into a few years of formal education. College is also a time when experimentation, and even failure, are possible and encouraged; a luxury most self-taught artists could never afford. Our experience tells us that almost everyone in high school who hopes to achieve a career in art and design would be advised to complete a college education first.

WHAT KIND OF DEGREE PROGRAM?

When thinking about an education in art and design, this question may be the most important, for it relates to the underlying purpose and philosophy of the program itself. To gain maximum advantage from your education, your own interests should closely match the intent of the college's program. Three kinds of degree programs are available to students choosing to study art and design: vocational, liberal arts, and professional.

Vocational Programs

Vocational programs are usually intended to prepare students for employment in entry-level jobs immediately after graduation. Virtually all of them lead to two-year degrees such as the Associate in Arts (AA) or the Associate in Applied Science (AAS). These are practical programs that usually place more emphasis on skills training than on liberal arts classes or higher-level conceptual work. They can often be helpful for students whose skill levels are not yet well-developed or who want to assess their commitment to art and design study. In most cases, these programs are available at public community colleges and thus are economical as well.

A difficulty with vocational programs, however, is that often they can be short and shortsighted, emphasizing immediate skills training and employment over the longer range educational needs that are generally part of four-year programs. Students with associates degrees have half the educational experiences compared with graduates of four year programs, and employers may be reluctant to hire them for anything other than the most basic tasks.

A variant on vocational programs at two-year schools are "transfer" programs. These prepare students for transfer to four-year colleges by matching the first two years of a typical four-year program. They can also be money savers (as long as the relationships between the two-year and four-year schools have been worked out to ensure a smooth transition) and can avoid many of the disadvantages of purely vocational programs mentioned above.

Liberal Arts Programs

These are four-year programs typically leading to a Bachelor of Arts (BA) degree. As the name implies, the liberal arts (general education of a nonprofessional or less specialized nature) are the focus of the curriculum, usually comprising about two-thirds of the course work. Art and design classes make up the remaining one-third of the course work. In an art program of this kind, a student completes about the same number of art classes as does a student in a two-year vocational program. Of course, they would take considerably more liberal arts (general education) classes.

Majoring in art in a liberal arts institution is ideal for students who want to attach as much liberal arts instruction as possible to their undergraduate art or design studies. This kind of program is also good for students who want to take a wide range of courses, while keeping their career options open as long as possible.

On the other hand, there are obviously less visual arts courses in this type of program, raising the same issues noted with two-year vocational programs—whether the amount of art and design course work is sufficient to prepare the student for more than basic work in the visual arts and to compete with others who have had a more extensive studio preparation.

Professional Programs

These, too, are four-year programs usually leading to a Bachelor of Fine Arts (BFA) degree. There are also a few professional colleges that offer the Bachelor of Science (BS) in some design disciplines, and a few that offer five-year degrees such as the Bachelor of Industrial Design (BID) or Bachelor of Graphic Design (BGD) degrees, all of which have goals and structures similar to the BFA degree. No matter what the designation, these programs emphasize significant study in the visual arts as a preparation for professional-level work in art and design fields. Visual arts classes will comprise roughly two-thirds of a student's course work, with liberal arts making up the remaining one-third of the courses.

It is impossible to obtain a bachelor's degree—whether a BA, BS, or BFA—without liberal arts courses. What distinguishes among undergraduate degree programs in the United States is the ratio between visual arts and liberal arts courses, and therefore the amount of emphasis placed on art and design study over four years. As you might assume, in a professional degree, this ratio of art and design to liberal arts classes is almost exactly the reverse of what is offered in a liberal arts-based program.

For students with a strong interest and ability in art and design, a professional degree is usually the most attractive and natural choice. In most design fields, a BFA (or BS) degree has become accepted as the standard college preparation for future employment. In fine arts career areas, too, the BFA is now the most common. Even for students whose skills are relatively strong, but whose interest is not quite so certain, a professional degree program may be the best way to begin an exploration of the visual arts, for you are in the company of other talented students and have the best chance of seeing what the future might hold for you.

A possible disadvantage of a professional program is that the liberal arts represent a smaller proportion of the overall course of study. For students with a strong interest in liberal arts, the ratio just may be skewed too far toward studio work. The BFA is not a better degree than a BA, or vice versa; they are of equal importance and quality. Their value lies in the extent to which they reflect your own educational and career interests. The key, then, is to think a lot about what you want out of college and to pick the type of degree according to your goals.

A Word About Graduate Degrees

Because this book is oriented mainly toward high school students, we are focusing almost all of our attention on undergraduate studies. But it is worth noting that educational practice, like work itself, is evolving. A career in the visual arts now almost always requires a college education, and the BFA is becoming the accepted degree for entering these professions. Similarly, graduate degrees such as the Master of Fine Arts (MFA) are increasingly available and necessary.

Many design and commercial arts areas do not require advanced study beyond the BFA. In illustration and fashion design, for example, the MFA degree is virtually nonexistent. In graphic design, the MFA degree is rare, but gaining in popularity. And in fine arts areas such as painting and sculpture, the MFA is becoming quite common, and it is a requisite for teaching at any level. But graduate study is a subject big enough for a separate book.

WHAT KIND OF COLLEGE?

Students really have two types of decisions to make when considering a college education. The kind of degree you select will determine the goals and the content of the curriculum you experience in college, particularly the relationship between liberal arts and studio art and design classes. The kind of college you select will have great affect on the social and environmental aspects of college, such as the nature of the student body and the college campus. For most college-bound students, curriculum content will be the major factor in college choice, particularly for those entering more specialized fields. Nevertheless, some students are concerned mainly with less academic issues, in which case campus style and atmosphere will override curricular concerns.

A major question is whether to pursue a BFA degree at a specialized art and design college or at the art department of a more general college or university. For a majority of students interested in art and design careers, the intensity and concentration of a specialized art and design college is the only choice. They feel they can learn more about art and design in this highly focused setting. For other students, a more wide-ranging environment with students majoring in many different subjects is more to their liking. This is a personal as well as an educational choice—and a tough choice as well.

Sound statistical research about whether students do better in their careers after graduating from one kind of college or another is hard to find, but a number of general statements can be made about this choice. One truth about a specialized art college is that its programs do not have to compete with other divisions of a large campus for attention and resources, nor are there layers of campus administration to go through when making changes to the curriculum. Change can often be implemented more rapidly at specialized colleges, whereas at larger and more complex universities, making changes or obtaining funds can take considerably more time. A college's ability to quickly change its program and structure in reaction to changes in the art and design fields is a notable asset today.

It is also true that the vast majority of the students at specialized colleges are quite committed to their choice of an art and design career, and thus can be intensely focused on their studio work. It is in the nature of specialized colleges to attract highly motivated art students. At a general liberal arts college, on the other hand, student interests can be quite varied, with some students highly committed to art practice and study while others are only marginally interested. A strength of these general colleges is the variety in disciplines offered, with students taking many different kinds of majors within the same college. This more wide-ranging campus may be exactly what some students are looking for in their college years, but it may not appeal to highly directed art and design students.

Professional art and design colleges have a wider range of art and design courses to choose from, since this is primarily what they teach. On the other hand, such colleges are likely to have a more limited choice of liberal arts classes and nonart electives, without the larger institution on which to draw. General colleges and universities can offer classes in many more departments outside the art and design curriculum, so choice in nonart subjects is increased considerably.

It is important to remember, however, that the number of liberal arts classes in a bachelor's degree program will be determined by the type of degree and not by the type of college in which you are enrolled. A larger, more broadly structured liberal arts college may have a wider choice of liberal arts courses

but requires no more of those courses for a four-year BFA than does a specialized art and design college. A BFA degree must have a certain ratio of liberal arts courses to studio courses, no matter what kind of college offers it.

There is also the issue of campus size to consider, whether you are considering an art college or a liberal arts college. On average, larger colleges tend to have larger classes and higher student–faculty ratios. Conversely, smaller colleges tend to have smaller classes and lower student-faculty ratios. Smaller campuses—whether art and design or liberal arts colleges—will almost always provide a more intimate setting and more personal attention. And larger schools often can be impersonal places, where a student can be "lost in the crowd."

An additional point is that larger institutions will usually offer, in addition to a larger selection of courses, a wider variety of activities and support services, which many students desire. If this interests you, you should also

be aware that many small or specialized colleges have formal exchange programs or cooperative arrangements with larger nearby colleges. This affords students the possibility of attending a smaller college while simultaneously gaining some of the services available at larger institutions. These arrangements often involve academic exchanges as well, so students may be able to get a wider range of liberal arts courses at the same time.

In the end, these are all personal issues; there are trade-offs, which only you can measure for yourself. A significant number of highly motivated art and design students feel that only an intense, professional, focused setting like an independent art and design college has the proper combination of students, faculty and curriculum for success in their chosen career. Other art students manage to fit in well in the art departments of universities or liberal arts colleges.

THE ADMISSIONS PROCESS

While there are almost as many admissions procedures as there are colleges, a few generalities can be presented here that will cover the majority of situations. But first, we'd like to repeat the advice we gave at the start of this book: relax and don't worry. College admissions competition has escalated lately to the point that it creates needless anxiety for everyone involved, especially the students. The reality is that there is a college—indeed a right college—for everyone who wants to attend. Of course, it is important to attend as good a college as possible, but the qualitative differences among the colleges most students apply to are not terribly large. Attending your second choice instead of your first choice college will not ruin your life. Attending the wrong college for you, however, may be costly.

The most important thing is that you look for the college that matches your needs and goals, not someone else's idea of what is important. This means being candid about what you care about in a college, what kind of campus environment you wish to spend four years in, and what you think you want to do with your life. In-person campus tours, sitting in on classes, even spending a night in the dorm, can provide invaluable insight into the nature of the colleges you are considering. We recommend that this phase of the admissions process—thinking about what you want and learning as much as possible about your colleges —receive your primary attention.

Specialized art and design colleges will invariably require you to submit your cumulative academic record and a portfolio of your art work. Many will also require an essay and your recent SAT/ACT scores. Most will advise a personal interview, if at all possible, and a few will require it for those within a certain distance from campus. In general, the same applies to art and design programs within liberal arts colleges and universities. However, for some colleges the student applies to the college first and then to the art program later on, so a portfolio may not be necessary at the first-year entry level. Read their catalogs carefully for these details.

The portfolio, like college admissions in general, causes great anxiety for applicants as well. And, like admissions anxiety, most of this stress is unnecessary. Your "portfolio" is simply a small collection of your recent work. There is no magic threshold that qualifies it as a portfolio; if you have work you have a portfolio. The primary purpose of a portfolio is to show your skills, creativity, interests, ambition, and commitment.

There is no simple prescription for content that will assure your acceptability, however, and showing a high level of motivation can easily overcome a limited art background. Schools rarely have a formulaic approach to the portfolio; rather, they want to see generally how you have developed thus far and what you may be capable of in the future. A few colleges (check the catalogs) may also require a small, formal "home test" to get specific kinds of work they are interested in and to overcome the wide variances they see in applicant portfolios and educational backgrounds.

Most schools are keen to see drawing, since it is a basic form of visual communication. You are almost always better off drawing directly from life (observation) than from a photograph. Beyond that, your portfolio should contain some breadth of artworks which show that you have worked in several different media or subjects. It should also reflect your own personal direction to the extent you have developed one. If you are very interested in one aspect of art or design, then you should have more of that in your portfolio. And

conversely, if your interests range widely, then a more general presentation is appropriate. It is not necessary to show "one of everything" in your portfolio, but it is important to show general art ability and to reflect your own personal interests. Also, for those schools where there is no common first-year Foundation program or for students entering above the first-year level, a more focused portfolio is expected.

If you feel you need portfolio counseling, National Portfolio Days (see Chapter 3) are a good way to get a preliminary, "no-obligation" review of your work and an assessment of your admissions potential. Most colleges are also happy to hold a personal informational session with you, and to talk about your work and their expectations. Most professional colleges and art departments will also offer summer or weekend courses tailored specifically to high school students, and these are good ways to build your experience and portfolio (a few schools actually offer specific "portfolio classes"). Finally, remember that if you have any questions, by all means contact the admissions staff directly. They are there to help you!

Here too, stress and anxiety are prevalent. The media are full of stories about colleges costing nearly $40,000 annually, including room and board. While a few rather high-priced colleges make for good headlines, the reality is that the vast majority of colleges are not nearly that expensive. The average independent art college tuition in 1999–2000 is about $15,000, with a range of about $10,000 to $20,000 being common, and this applies to most private colleges and universities in the United States The typical public college or university will have a tuition of anywhere from $2,000 to as much as $10,000. The costs of room and board, travel, art supplies, and books at all these colleges are not terribly different from each other—it is mainly tuition that distinguishes the "cost of attendance" at public and private colleges.

One of the earliest mistakes students and parents can make in the admissions process is to assume that a certain college, or a certain kind of college, is out of reach financially, by focusing on the "nominal price" (the stated full tuition) rather than the "net price" (after financial aid has been applied). Virtually every college in the United States offers financial aid, and some offer a considerable amount. Students owe it to themselves not to narrow their choices too early in the process; not to eliminate colleges before they have found out how much financial aid is available. Often, the most expensive colleges offer the most financial aid, meaning that the highest "sticker price" can turn out to be the most affordable option. Attending almost any college will take some sacrifice (cutting expenses, taking out loans, etc.), but only after you have received your full financial aid packages from each college that you are interested in can you make an accurate and informed decision about cost.

Most colleges will offer numerous kinds of aid, based either on merit or need, or both. In addition, there are local, state, federal, and other private sources an eligible student can apply to for financial assistance. College catalogs list all the various types of aid available, and you will also find similar information in the many financial aid guide books available in bookstores everywhere. Ultimately, almost all college financial aid will come either from or through the colleges themselves, so we strongly advise that you work closely with the financial aid offices throughout your application process.

ONCE YOU ENTER COLLEGE

By now you have surely picked up on a theme running through this book—we think you should do less worrying, do a lot of research, think things out carefully, make some decisions, but then not be afraid to change your mind. It is rare to have enough information (about yourself or a college or a career) or to make a perfect decision in this beginning stage of career development. All things change, including your goals, talents, and self-awareness, and you are always learning. If you develop strong new interests or talents down the road and you want to pursue them, by all means do so—many of the people we profile in the following pages have done just that.

Web sites offering advice on financial aid have sprouted up all over the Internet, although many are often trying to sell you a book or search service at the same time. We strongly recommend <www.finaid.org> over other sites. In our opinion this is the most balanced and thorough Web site pertaining to financial aid. We particularly encourage you to read the sections at <www.finaid.org> pertaining to scholarship search services and avoid those that charge a fee for what is readily available for free.

Careers & Profiles

CHAPTER 2

Photos by Todd Hido

This portion of the book presents information on nearly 30 different career areas in art and design. After some introductory remarks, we present brief descriptions of the various fields, followed by profiles of professionals in those fields. These artists and designers are alumni of the colleges that belong to AICAD, the organization which publishes this book. Please realize that there is much more available at all these schools than just the fields represented by the alumni we have selected to profile here.

Trying to narrow art and design practice in the United States down to 30 categories and 40 individuals overly simplifies the incredible scope of what can be done with an art and design education. However, to keep the size of this book under control, we have clustered a few related areas together, even though some colleges or practitioners will title them differently. Because we could not present every possible variant on each career area, you are encouraged to speak further with the colleges that interest you, and even seek out professionals and faculty in these fields for more information.

You will notice that many people profiled here have changed or evolved in the years since they were in college. This is a common occurrence in the art and design world; people often wander into adjacent areas or even begin an entirely new art activity. So as you review these careers, please be aware that the boundaries between them are not rigid or impermeable— movements and combinations are always taking place.

Because of this moving and evolving, it is almost always helpful to have a solid foundation (both in liberal arts and visual arts) before specializing in one specific field. Now more than ever, with the world becoming more complex and interconnected and as more people work in interdisciplinary teams, the liberal arts and a broad art experience contribute greatly to your ability to understand the visual and social world, to remain flexible throughout your lifetime, and to work with others.

In spite of how specialized, particular or narrow some of these fields may appear, they all have their roots in the same basics of visual language. Drawing, color, composition, and form are universal skills in all art and design career areas. Even in something like computer animation— where there is often the assumption that computers do all the work—it is humans who draw everything (the computer is just another medium or tool) and usually the computer isn't even used until well into the process of story development.

WORK AND EARNINGS

We often receive inquiries about which career area will ensure the greatest security or income. The short answer is "the one which you do best and enjoy most." One career area may pay more than others, but if you are not highly talented in that particular career area then you probably will not earn much compared to an outstanding person in a supposedly lower paying field. In the end, you have to follow your talent and your interests.

Future employment estimates from the Department of Labor indicate that most visual arts fields will enjoy healthy job growth in the next decade. This is especially true of art education and computer-related activities.

But with all aspects of design becoming ever more central to our lives (as told in a recent "Time Magazine" cover story) and with information and communication becoming heavily visual, it would appear that talented artists and designers will have generally good employment prospects.

As a rule, the fine arts and crafts are less geared towards regular full-time employment, so their security and earning potential are generally lower than careers in design (commercial art) areas. On the other hand, the world is full of exceptions to the rule—painters or photographers who are extremely successful and well-paid, and commercial artists who always struggle to make ends meet.

Design areas often look attractive because of these salary and security issues. But in these fields you are almost always working for others— clients. You have their problems to solve, their needs to consider, and their deadlines to follow. Consequently, there can be less freedom and flexibility in such endeavors. Fine artists almost always work for only one person—themselves. They have only their own direction and ideas to pursue. Crafts can often straddle these two formats, working both for themselves and for clients as well.

The rewards and the feedback in design areas can be more immediate, as well. Artists and craftspersons may work for years before knowing how well their work will be received. In addition, fine arts and crafts are often solitary activities, involving a single person in a studio. Design can involve individuals working on a freelance basis, but much more often means working in an office or with a team of other people.

As suggested earlier, many of these fields can be undertaken as both a fine art and a commercial art. Photography, for example, can lead to photojournalism or straight commercial work, but it is also a fine arts area where personal vision is central and there is no "client." The same applies to areas like film, video, furniture design, or computer art. Drawing is often shown as a fine art in galleries, but also can be commercial when applied to the field of illustration. Many of the artists and designers profiled in this chapter will frequently cross over between a fine art and a commercial art orientation.

In the end, the key to a successful career (beyond the basic ingredients of energy and commitment) is to pick a field of study that closely matches your own strengths and interests.

This is a deeply personal choice requiring considerable introspection. And, as we have said before, if you have some indecision, make the best choice you can at the time it is necessary and then stay flexible and open to all possibilities.

GENERAL DEFINITIONS

There is a wide variety of words and phrases used to discuss the fields of art and design, and the differences between some of them are matters of nuance only. Traditionally, "fine art" refers to those areas that are derived from and motivated by personal expression, without the involvement of a direct "client" or a commercial purpose. These include painting, drawing, sculpture, printmaking, photography, film, video, performance, and related areas. A close relative is "crafts," which typically include ceramics, jewelry, woodworking, and textiles, and all their variants. Crafts often have a more utilitarian and commercial purpose (hand-woven clothing, earrings, etc.), and many times are produced in multiples. But the border between it and the fine arts is porous. Many sculptures are made of clay, while many photographs or prints are made in multiples.

**Dr Katz,
Professional Therapist**
Annette LeBlanc Cate, 1996

"Design" areas are often also called applied art (art images "applied" to a commercial purpose become "illustration" for example) or commercial art. Here, there is almost always a client for which the design is done and a specific commercial result—such as an ad campaign, an office plan, or a corporate logo. The fact that the work is not "fine art" does not mean it isn't expressive or inventive; all design needs to be creative. The difference is that in design the impetus for the work is external rather than internal, and the result is intended to be commercial. In fine arts and crafts, the work created is usually sold (a "commercial" result) when it is finished. However, except for specific commissions, it is usually not created for a client.

Animation and Computer Animation

Animation is the process of drawing sequential pictures which, when assembled, form a moving image over time. In the past, this work was done by hand with teams of artists creating literally thousands of drawings for a cartoon, ad, or film. These days, more and more animation work is done on a computer which can speed up the process while also increasing the complexity of the images and the lengths of a film. Consequently, there has been an explosion in the field of animation, with many more people employed in it now than ever before. Strong, facile drawing skill is a must for entry into this field, as is an ability to work on the same project for an extended period of time with a team of other artists.

Architecture

Architecture is the process of creating the three-dimensional spaces we live and work in—ranging from houses to schools to offices to stores. The work involves a combination of creativity, spatial ability, drawing skill, and knowledge of materials, structures and construction methods. There are many good books written about architecture so we have not profiled that field here. In the Resources chapter of this book, you will find contact information for the Association of Collegiate Schools of Architecture (ACSA), which publishes an excellent guide to the study of architecture. We also recommend the book "Architect: A Candid Guide to the Profession", by Roger K. Lewis, MIT Press.

Art Direction

Art Direction is a branch of graphic and communication design which has an over-arching aspect to it. Art Directors are, in a sense, visual choreographers, seeing to all aspects of large-scale graphic projects. Magazines, television stations, and most large corporations usually employ Art Directors to ensure consistency, creativity, and an overall "look" for all the visual products created by the company. Art Directors almost always start their careers in graphic design or commercial art, and then combine that ability with good management skills. Leadership skills are also necessary, because an Art Director is usually supervising teams of artists, designers, and photographers.

Art Education

Art Education is a field that combines your visual skills and teaching ability to help students of all ages learn art and design. A large portion of this field works in the K-12 arena, where a solid and relatively broad visual education is required in order to cover a wide range of subjects for all students. There is also considerable teaching taking place in colleges and universities, museums, and community centers across the country. Salaries and working formats will vary accordingly in this field. Most formal teaching jobs will require graduate degree as well. Over the next decade there is expected to be a very large demand for K-12 art teachers, as the school-age population increases and current, older faculty retire. (Art Therapy is a related field in which a specific graduate degree is required.)

Cartooning

Cartooning is the creation of stylized or simplified drawings for the purpose of telling a story, making a point, or making people laugh. One form of this work is the editorial or humor cartoon, such as seen on the Op-Ed pages of newspapers or in magazines such as the "New Yorker." Another familiar form is the comic book; dramatic or fantastic stories told through a series of drawings. Good drawing skill obviously is essential in this field, as is an ability to make those drawings expressive and engaging.

Ceramics and Clay

As we suggested at the start of this chapter, ceramics is an area with many outlets. It can range from exquisite, complicated single pieces of sculpture to useful mass-produced household items. Clay can be manipulated in ways that most people cannot imagine. No matter what the end product, working with this material involves not just a solid three-dimensional ability, but a technical knowledge of how clay and glazes function.

Computer Graphics and Digital Imaging

Unlike other art forms, computer art is a relatively new development, paralleling the rise of the personal computer starting in the mid-80s. The recent dramatic increase in computing power has made this technology ubiquitous in our daily lives and in art and design fields. Digital design was once limited to graphics and publishing, and often functioned as simply a faster and more mechanical version of traditional graphic design. But over the last decade, the field has evolved to stand on its own as a distinct area of work, and now also involves new and interactive media as well (see that career area on p.19). Regardless of the technology used, electronic art has as its foundation the same skills in composition, color, typography, and communication as all other areas of design.

Drawing

Drawing is probably be the oldest art form in existence. Today, it is not only a basic means of communication and idea development among artists and designers, but still an fine art form in its own right. Like painting and photography, it can be an expressive and personal, communicative and provocative, colorful and varied.

Environmental Design

Environmental Design is an area that extends interior design in broader directions, often with elements of architecture and graphic design included. As the name implies, it involves creating the entire environment of a space, whether inside or outside. Much of this work is in commercial projects, where it may cover lighting, signage, traffic patterns, furniture, and much more—in short, anything that shapes a space for human use. Three-dimensional and spatial abilities are key in this field, as is an understanding of social and human processes.

Fashion Design

The simple definition of fashion design is that it is the invention of the clothes we all wear all the time. However, that does little justice to the complexity and creativity involved in bringing clothes to the marketplace. Fashion design involve a sensitivity to tastes and trends, to construction techniques and fabric characteristics, and to shape and color. It is the process of drawing these various components together to create something new and exciting for people to wear. This work can be done on a relatively small and personal scale, where the designer can be responsive to the individual customer. Or it can range up to the sophisticated and large-scale activities of Seventh Avenue, where life can be hectic and competitive. Good drawing and color skills, plus a knowledge of fabric and form, are essential.

Film and Video

Like many other areas of art and design, film and video can encompass a wide range of formats and approaches. At one end of the spectrum are fine arts-oriented films and videos. At the other end are full-scale Hollywood productions such as "Good Will Hunting" (directed by Gus Van Sant, a graduate of Rhode Island School of Design). And in between those are video installations, independent films, documentaries, and many other variants of the same media. Accordingly, describing the work environment in these areas is rather difficult, since it covers such a wide territory. Imagination and technical knowledge are pre-requisites here.

Fine Arts

Fine arts is really a huge area encompassing almost everything that artists create for themselves. We have given it a separate heading in order to focus on aspects of fine art that do not easily fit into the standard categories of painting, sculpture, and so on. The fine artists featured here have found new ways to combine various aspects of fine arts or have created entirely new avenues for their own work, all of it growing from a solid visual arts foundation. For all of them, fine arts is an expressive process, a way to say things or to provide commentary on our daily lives.

RIGHT
Thunderbird Concept,
Ford Motor Co.
Jay Mays, 1999

BELOW RIGHT
Presbyterian Church Logo
Malcolm Grear

Furniture Design and Woodworking

As with Ceramics on p.16, this is an area that can range from single objects in a crafts or fine arts mode, to mass-produced pieces sold through commercial showrooms. Much of the work, particularly in smaller quantities, is done in wood, while the more commercial work is often produced in metal and plastic as well. This field requires a thorough knowledge of the materials being used, coupled with a strong three-dimensional ability.

Glass and Glass Blowing

Here too, as with other crafts areas, work in this field ranges from individual, personal "fine art" pieces to large-scale projects and multiple pieces for commercial clients. Similarly, the employment opportunities cover the same wide range. In glass, the artist's visual abilities (color and form) combine with a technical knowledge of how the material performs during use.

Graphic Design and Communication Design

This is one of the largest and most diverse of all the visual fields. Often called graphic design, it is now frequently referred to as communication design or visual communications, to more fully suggest the central role of communication in this field of work. Graphic design can cover virtually anything—including ads, magazines, signage, Web site, packages, or corporate identity systems—that involves combining words and images to communicate something to others. A strong sense of composition and color are essential, but so is experience in communication theory, sociology, and problem-solving. Some professionals in this field work on their own in a free-lance mode, although many work with others in offices (large or small) for corporate clients. (See also "Computer Graphics" on p.16.)

Illustration

Illustration is the process of applying an image (usually drawing or painting) to a communications problem, usually for an outside client. Great skill in drawing and painting are central to this area of work. Projects can range from Op-Ed illustrations, to drawings for ad campaigns, to images that accompany magazine articles.

Illustration is a relatively diverse field—it can come quite close to graphic design, in that it can sometimes involve the use of typography and page layouts, and it also can come quite close to fine arts in that a drawing or painting may be nearly indistinguishable from non-commercial work.

Industrial Design and Product Design

Industrial or product design combines a technical/mechanical ability with skills in three-dimensional art and problem-solving, to create objects that answer customer and client needs. As a recent cover story in Time Magazine demonstrated, the designer can touch all aspects of our daily lives. Cars, household appliances, medical equipment, computers—nearly any three-dimensional object—can benefit from and be improved with designer input. As with graphic design, work in this field can be varied; solo and freelance-based, or part of a larger design firm.

Interior Design and Interior Architecture

Interior design and interior architecture touch on virtually every aspect of the shape, color, and usefulness of interior spaces. Although often thought of as limited to residential design, in fact much of the field is involved with commercial design for offices, stores and institutions. This design work requires knowledge of lighting, furniture, manufacturing and materials, regulations such as the Americans With Disabilities Act (ADA), computer aided design (CAD), and specialized client needs. As with most other design areas, the settings can range from single-person practices to large, diverse offices with many designers.

Multi-Media and New Media

This is a broad, new, evolving area incorporating combinations of computers, video, television, and interactive media. As a field with somewhat blurred boundaries, it has some basis in the fine arts but mainly makes use of design skills and computers. Communication is usually at the center of this work, so students are aided by a knowledge of graphic design and visual theory, as well as computer software.

Metals and Jewelry

Like the other crafts areas described earlier, light metals and jewelry offer many possibilities for working and creating. Some people concentrate on making unique objects for a single customer, while others move into larger-scale designs for a wider market, such as mass-produced jewelry or table settings. The work settings parallel this format, ranging from single-artist studios to larger companies. But in all cases, a knowledge of the materials must combine with a sophisticated sense of form and style.

New Genre and Performance

This field first appeared in the 1960s as a melding of sculpture and theater, driven by artists who wanted to escape the static limitations of the pure sculptural object. It has now expanded further to encompass site installations and video and almost any other new medium, and so remains a diverse and fluid area of the fine art. Some work created in this area is quite temporary; that is, it may only exist for the duration of the performance itself, with only the memory of the experience lingering. Other work is more lasting and is now being collected by museums and galleries. It is often humorous, often challenging, and almost always "tells a story."

Painting

One of the oldest art forms, painting is constantly evolving as a means of investigation and expression. This field captures the full range of visual expression, from assembled, built-up, large-scale, almost three-dimensional abstract works, to traditional figurative oil paintings, and everything imaginable in between. Almost always this is a solitary undertaking, involving considerable time alone in the studio. Like other fine art forms, success and fame can come quickly to some people or they can be elusive and slow to arrive for other artists. In the end, regardless of remuneration, it is the pleasure and the challenge of visual expression that drives all painters.

Photography

Photography is the process of fixing an image in time. In the past, this was done on a piece of film exactly as the artist saw it. Now, however, many artists also alter and manipulate their photographs, or use digital cameras and other new technology to produce all manner of images from light. As a field, photography is also quite varied, ranging from fine arts-based work that appears in galleries to commercial photography and photo-journalism. Naturally, employment opportunities are just as varied.

Printmaking

Printmaking—whether intaglio, lithography, silkscreen, woodcuts, or other formats—is a process of transferring a drawing to a form of relief and then to multiple hand-made images. At its core is drawing and color, although photography is often used now as well. As with other fine arts media, this is a personal and expressive art form driven by the artist's individual interests. Work is usually sold through galleries and other commercial venues, and will also appear in museums.

Sculpture

Sculpture is fine arts work executed in three-dimensions. It can be large or small, personal or political, realistic or abstract, but it is always about manipulating material (mass) and the space around it. Galleries or museums are typical avenues for showing this work, but sculptors can often support themselves with private and public commissions of their work. An understanding of form and color and spatial relationships is critical to this endeavor.

Textiles and Fibers

This area can range from screen printing on flat textiles, to weaving with threads and yarns on a loom, to assembling three-dimensional pieces with various fibers, and from unique crafts pieces, to commissioned constructions, to large-scale textile manufacturing. It almost always involves use of color and composition, and may be done in connection with furniture or interior designers as well. Employment opportunities range from individual craftsperson to commercial designer.

Transportation Design

Transportation design is a specialized offshoot of industrial or product design. Although often thought of as simply car design, this area of study now is broadening to include other forms of transportation such as motorcycles, buses, recreational vehicles, and even bicycles. It combines some mechanical and practical knowledge with artistic three-dimensional abilities. The work is most often with corporations, either as a staff designer or as a consultant to those corporations.

Other Specializations and Related Fields

Some areas of art and design are quite specialized and rare, and therefore are not given a full profile in this publication. This would include areas such as art administration or gallery administration and museum studies, which combine art or art history knowledge with administrative or management skills. Medical Illustration (drawing and painting in service to the medical professions) is another highly specialized area offered by only a handful of schools. Toy design is a new and growing area—previously related only to traditional children's toys, it now includes computer and interactive game design. Many artists and designers also move into tangential areas such as theater, music, art history and criticism, and creative writing.

Animation and Computer Animation

JEFF PRATT

TOP & BELOW
Geri's Game,
Pixar Animation
Studios, 1997

"The impact of Feature Animation on society is amazing. To see 5- and 6- year old children clutching a Woody doll from "Toy Story" as they walk down the street or hear them repeat lines from movies, shows that that person will always deeply remember that movie throughout his or her life, and the messages that the film contained. Animated films have the power to not only entertain, but to reach people of all walks of life in manner that no other medium can."

Jeff Pratt began his professional career as a mechanical engineer working for NASA. He was responsible for the testing and check-out of Space Shuttle Mechanical Systems to prepare for flight turnaround. He also spent time working on environmental control and life support systems. He left this profession in 1992 to attend the Ringling School of Art and Design in Florida majoring in Graphic Design and minoring in Computer Animation.

Today, Jeff is a character animator for Pixar Animation Studios in California. He has worked on the full-length animated feature films "Toy Story" (working with a team of 28 other artists), "A Bugs Life," and "Toy Story 2," and the short film "Geri's Game" (which won an Oscar in 1998). He is now in pre-production for Pixar's next full-length animated feature film.

His education at Ringling provided him with the opportunity to develop his potential future as a Computer Animator as he wrestled in deciding which direction he wanted his professional career to go. His education gave him the hands-on experience to allow him to go directly from school into his new occupation. His animation courses provided him the knowledge and expertise to master the various computer animation software programs used in the industry.

ANNETTE LEBLANC CATE

"Contrary to what many people might think, just because something is called 'computer animation' doesn't mean it is computer-created. On the Dr. Katz show, every image was drawn by hand on the computer."

Born in Waltham, Massachusetts, Annette attended the Art Institute of Boston (AIB) graduating with a combined major in Fine Arts and Illustration. Her first job was for Tom Snyder Productions, an educational software firm, as an art assistant where she did illustration and animation for a children's video series. She and Tom then developed "Squigglevision," a low-cost computer animation process that is now used for television.

Later, as the Senior Art Director for Tom Snyder Productions, Annette lead the team responsible for the "Dr. Katz, Professional Therapist" show that ran for six years on Comedy Central and won a Cable Ace Award for animation. Annette's responsibilities included the entire "look" of the show, designing both the characters and backgrounds, and all the details of how they would appear to viewers. She hired and trained all the artists, managed the day-to-day running of the show and ensured that all deadlines were met. The series was voted one of the top ten TV shows by "TV Guide" magazine in 1996. Annette served as the Art Director for the show's entire run while also continuing to do illustrations for the show.

Annette is currently working on developing the look for a new children's TV show. She also enjoys doing freelance illustration for such magazines as Cobblestone and Cricket, working in pen and ink and watercolor. She hopes to one day design characters and backgrounds for animated movies.

Annette credits her strong drawing skills to her time at AIB. In her chosen profession of computer animation, Annette uses everything she learned about design, composition and color everyday. In many ways, Annette says, "creating an animated TV show is just like one gigantic illustration project after another....Each scene is like a separate page in a book, with its own composition problems to consider. Characters have to fit into the background, it all has to make sense and it all has to look good. And, it all has to be done very quickly." Art college also taught her the value of teamwork—"these projects are about teamwork and the ability to communicate."

TOP
Dr Katz, Professional Therapist, 1996

LEFT
A Feast Fit for a Fish, 1995

ARTIST PHOTO
by Robert Cate

Art Direction

TODD GILMOUR

A 1990 graduate of the Pratt Institute, Todd currently works as the Chief Designer for Smart-Money's education division. Prior to this, Todd worked for Standard and Poor's Published Image as design director, and before that as graphic designer for the design firms Scudder, Stevens & Clark, and Smith & Hemingway.

When asked to define his career, Todd says that he has been a designer, art director, design director, and chief designer. But he feels that you can replace all those labels with the general title of "creative contributor." While working for Published Image, Todd was responsible for the design of all print collateral.

When at S&P Published Image, the company decided to move its location and Todd asked to work with the architects in conceptualizing the new loft space to which the firm was relocating. Although way outside of his job description, Todd didn't want to confine himself to the role of print designer, so he took a chance and, as he said, "it was a blast." Had he thought of himself as only a print designer he would have missed out on what turned out to be, "an amazing opportunity working with an entirely differently creative team."

Todd credits his art teacher at his magnet arts high school for his success today. Her portfolio-building program prepared to him to enter college. Pratt in turn provided an environment that facilitated students interacting with professionals, not just professors preparing him for the real world creative challenges. He also found great value in the college's critique sessions. They helped him formulate and express valid opinions supporting choices of color, composition, type and materials.

TOP
S+P Published Image,
loft space, 1998

LEFT
The Independent Advisor for DPM

FAR LEFT
Portfolio Edge,
Standard & Poors, 1999

"I think consumers are more conscious of design today than ever in the past. Strong design is recognized as a valuable attribute. Producers have recognized it, and in response, are employing designers to develop new products like Apple's iMac, Volkswagen's new Beetle, and publications like "Wallpaper" and "Fast Company." I'm very excited about the future and can't wait to see what lies ahead."

CARL LOPES

"Jobs in art education continue to grow as second-ary schools and colleges integrate the arts into their curriculum base. Art education impacts our society more today than ever before. Improved world-wide economical commerce, diverse tech-nological multi-media communications, and heightened aesthetic demand require more and more instructors skilled in the arts."

An art teacher on Cape Cod, Massachusetts, Carl is a gradu-ate of the Pratt Institute. He is Director of Art for Barnstable High School's Art & Applied Technology Department. His teaching skills are to be admired. In 1998, 15 of his students won awards in the regional Scholas-tic Art Awards competition sponsored by the "Boston Globe." Carl was recently quoted as saying, "Our program has grown tremendously. Many of our students are graduating and going onto some really great art colleges."

He has an obvious passion for teaching, but says he also enjoys the job because it allows him the summers off to spend with his family and to devote eight hours a day to his love of painting. He is an accomplished and well-respected painter who exhibits his work through-out New England. His painting is described as striking geometrical abstractions; a contemporary study of tonal changes and space relationships.

His Pratt education prepared him to be technically skilled and well versed in many studio art areas. "A person cannot teach to others what he/she has not gained experience or expertise in." He believes it is crucial for an art educator to be proficient, skillful, creative and talented as an artist. He also believes that an artist who teaches must be able to impart well what he knows to students individually and in group settings. He sees teaching as a people-based

occupation that requires extreme flexibility and sensitivity. He says that from a social context his occupation is both "highly rewarding and occasionally frus-trating." But, all in all, he finds being an art educator a privilege.

TOP
Theatriques, 1997

ABOVE
Diatonics, 1995

LEFT
Modulations, 1996

JOHN P. HART

PRINCE VALIANT AND THE
KNIGHTS OF THE ROUND
TABLE HAVE SCARCELY
RETURNED TO TINTAGEL
WHEN A NEW PLEA FOR
HELP ARISES. THE
CHRONICLES REPORT
THAT PRINCE VALIANT
AND ALETA CAN ENJOY
BUT A FEW AUTUMNAL
DAYS IN EACH OTHER'S
COMPANY.

TOP
Nude, 1999

ABOVE & BELOW
line art for **Prince Valiant**
comic strip, 1999

ARTIST PHOTO
Diane Aeschliman

VAL MARVELS AT HOW A
LOVE THAT BEGAN IN FRAGILE
AND SOMETIMES PAINFULLY
VIVID COLORS HAS MATURED
INTO SOMETHING STRONGER
AND MORE POWERFUL.

"The human form will always endure in art. It defines who we are as a society, how we function, what we understand. The figure must continue to be taught with authority, crafted with mastery, and used by artists of every nature to communicate the limitless encounters of our human journey."

Self-described as coming from the potato fields of eastern Idaho, John P. Hart, developed an early love for drawing and painting. He received his "first commission" in fifth grade when asked to paint the schoolhouse by his principal. By the sixth grade, John taught watercolor to younger students. Feeling unprepared "to take on the world" after high school, John attended a local community college and earned an AAS degree in fine art. Feeling more secure in his talents, John then headed east to the Lyme Academy of Fine Arts in Connecticut and graduated in 1999.

Today, John is working as an assistant to John Cullen Murphy, the artist who creates the Sunday comic strip "Prince Valiant." He prepares the preliminary compositions and inkings for many of the storyboards going to publications in 350 Sunday newspapers worldwide. He sees this as a marvelous opportunity, as he gets to work directly with Mr. Murphy whom he considers an old-school master of the human form.

John is also focusing his attention on another of his passions in an MFA program in Medical Illustration at the University of Michigan. He hopes to use his education to work with doctors and surgeons who are pushing the boundaries of our knowledge of the human body. It is his desire to effectively employ a greater understanding of the human body in his work, whether in creating his own figurative

compositions, or Prince Valiant drawings, or medical illustrations, or teaching the next generation of figurative artists.

John's education was invaluable to the work he performs today. He feels that without the study and the mentors he found at Lyme, his career would not have progressed to the point it is now and the direction it seems to be heading. The study of the human form provided John the foundation to build his career upon and the mentors helped him to overcome some of the obstacles in choosing to become an artist. He credits art college with facilitating his connections to the working world.

Ceramics and Clay

AKIO TAKAMORI

"Already, clay is playing an important role as an art material because of its accessibility and rich historical tradition. The material, which you can manipulate directly with your hands, will be increasingly desirable and important to counterbalance the fast growing high technological society."

Akio Takamori is a ceramic artist—a sculptor whose medium is clay. He graduated from the Kansas City Art Institute (KCAI) with a BFA degree in 1976. He went onto earn his MFA in ceramics in 1978. His work is represented in many public collections including the Carnegie Institute Art Museum, Los Angeles County Museum, American Craft Museum, Victoria and Albert Museum, Tacoma Art Museum and the Taipei Fine Arts Museum. He has been awarded the National Endowment for the Arts grant in 1986, 1988 and 1992.

Akio is an associate professor of Art in the Ceramics Department at the University of Washington. He lives and maintains a working studio in Seattle as well. In a practical sense, Akio defines his career as a studio artist and a professor, in that order. He sees his passion of creating ceramics as a continual progression of his life and of his life's work.

His educational experiences served to broaden his vision and taught him how to cultivate and refine the direction of his artwork. He believes that his time at KCAI gave him the ability to learn and employ a good work ethic and that this lesson continues to serve him in everything that he does today.

TOP
Sleeping Man with School Boy, 1999

ABOVE
Akio Takamori with **Installation of Figures,** 1998

LEFT **Installation of Figures,** 1999

ARTIST PHOTO
Eduardo Calderon

TED COFFMAN

Ted was born and reared in Dayton, Ohio. He had an interest in drawing from an early age and won several awards for his creative talents in high school. Before attending college, Ted worked many freelance jobs doing everything from sign painting to character design and development for educational board games to murals for private and commercial establishments. He then turned to construction work to support his wife and three children. At the age of 32 he applied for and was awarded a scholarship to Columbus College of Art and Design (CCAD). He sold his construction business, packed up his family and moved to Columbus, where he earned a BFA in Illustration.

A few months before graduating from CCAD, Ted was offered and accepted a job as Marketing Director for a Columbus design firm, but after only six months he was itching to branch out on his own. He started Coffman Studios and worked out of his own house. Although Ted had spent many years working in traditional illustration and fine arts media, he is now more involved with the Internet and creates web pages and computer graphic presentations for his clients. He believes that the task of creating imagery that communicates clearly to its audience has taken on new meaning with the emerging use of technology.

Ted acknowledges that there are some people who are successful at making a living in an art-related field without formal training, but for him school was of critical importance to his personal development. He knows how competitive the field of computer graphics is and how it will become even more so in the future. Ted once asked a professor in his freshman year at CCAD about employment opportunities for artists today. The professor replied, "look around you; an artist has in some way touched everything you see and use." He believes that this is and has always been a true statement. Securing a formal education was a vital step in assuring his professional development.

"Art will always be an integral part of society; therefore, to be an artist is one of the greatest honors, one of the greatest careers one could ever choose."

TOP
Isaac, 1998
LEFT
Darby Creek, 1998
ARTIST PORTRAIT
Ted Coffman

Computer Graphics and Digital Imaging

AGNIESZKA GASPARSKA

Agnieszka Gasparszka was born and raised in Warsaw, Poland until the age of 11, when she and her family moved to Queens, New York. Participating in the general panic that besets most seniors in high school, she applied to nine different colleges. Only one of those was an art college, which she almost didn't apply to because she, like many others, felt that an education, yet alone a career in art, was not a very practical thing to do. Well, she got into Cooper Union and it not only changed her life, but her perceptions about art and art careers.

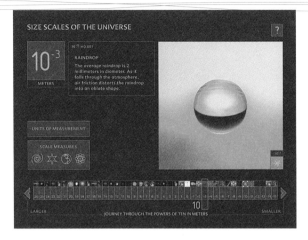

SIZE SCALES OF THE UNIVERSE

10^{-3}

METERS

$10^{-3} = 0.001$

RAINDROP
The average raindrop is 2 millimeters in diameter. As it falls through the atmosphere, air friction distorts the raindrop into an oblate shape.

UNITS OF MEASUREMENT

SCALE MEASURES

10

LARGER   JOURNEY THROUGH THE POWERS OF TEN IN METERS   SMALLER

TOP & LEFT
website for the
Museum of Natural History, 1999

BELOW LEFT
website for
1999 AIGA Conference

ARTIST PHOTO
Charlie Pizarello

"The impact of digital media on our culture is overwhelming these days. Considering how many people are involved in this digital culture—either using it or designing it—it is really important for people coming out of art schools to have the right skills and creative backgrounds to become a part of creating this community."

While attending Cooper Union, Agnieszka studied at the Ecole de Beaux Arts in Paris for a semester and also served as an assistant for a major exhibition produced by Cooper Union. In her senior year of college she got a part time job as a designer for Funny Garbage in New York, a design and production company specializing in CD-ROMs, Web, print and animation work. Now a recent graduate, she works for Funny Garbage full time as an Art Director. Her recent projects have included design of interactive information kiosks for the new Planetarium at the American Museum of Natural History in New York, and the Experience Music Project Museum in Seattle. Additionally, she has worked on Scooby.com—Scooby Doo's own

web site within the Cartoon Network—a web site for the American Institute of Graphic Arts Biennial Conference, a virtual tour of the Hanna Barbera Studios also for The Cartoon Network online, as well as a new website for Knoll Inc.

By studying many different disciplines at one time, Agnieszka feels that she opened herself up to a whole new way of looking at life. She believes she had a very well rounded education, which she didn't anticipate receiving at an art school. She also believes that our society is touched in countless ways by creativity and that her education helped her to develop her own creativity and eventually her career path.

Drawing

LARRY THOMAS

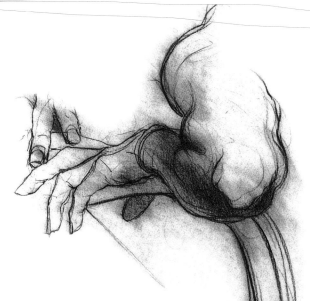

Larry's work is based on a commitment to being in his studio on a regular basis, supported by his teaching and administrative work. It is very important to Larry to balance his academic duties with his studio endeavors. He currently maintains a studio in Mendocino County, California, where he plans to take the 2001–2002 year to prepare for his next solo exhibit.

Larry's educational experience in art colleges provided him a solid foundation for his later work. His early development as an artist was supported and mentored by practicing teachers and artists who encouraged, stimulated, criticized and "pushed him" as a student. He sees art college as a period of exploration, investigation, and research in an environment where he could challenge established aesthetic conventions and attitudes. And he sees drawing as the best avenue to explore ideas and to conceptualize.

TOP
Owl Wing #4, 1986

LEFT & BELOW
Figure Studies, 1993

ARTIST PHOTO
Charles Kennard

Born in Memphis, Tennessee in 1943, Larry Thomas not only received a BFA from the Memphis College of Art and an MFA from the San Francisco Art Institute (SFAI), but today is the Dean of Academic Affairs at SFAI. In addition to contributing to the visual arts through his teaching and administrative duties, Larry's primary passion is drawing (although he also practices printmaking, calligraphy and sculpture as well). Larry has had countless group and solo exhibitions throughout the world for the past 25 years. He has also received a residency at the American Academy in Rome and two National Endowment for the Arts Fellowships, participated in a cultural delegation to Yunnan Province, China, and served as a visiting faculty or lecturer at more than a dozen colleges.

"I like drawing because it is immediate and portable. It helps me think through ideas and hone my own vision."

Environmental Design

BELOW
Michael Donovan's
**Texas Instruments
Sundial**
*Photo by Hedrich
Blessing Photography*

ARTIST PHOTOS
Amos Chan

NANCYE GREEN
AND MICHAEL DONOVAN

The story of Nancye and Michael is a story of professional success. They met just prior to graduation at Parsons School of Design where they both studied environmental design. Both attended other undergraduate schools before that: Nancye receiving a degree in Political Science from Newcomb College of Tulane University and Michael a degree from Iowa State University.

The two formed Donovan & Green 25 years ago, shortly after graduation. The firm specializes in environmental design. At first they worked extensively helping community groups reshape their environments—schools in particular. They opened their office, "taking on work that compelled us." They designed exhibits, showrooms, school curricula, multimedia events, and graphics. They look back on it as a very exciting time, constantly learning about how to design,

manage complex projects, and grow a business. Nancye says, "Our job was, in fact, designing a life and our work within it."

Their firm grew and evolved over many years. Then, in 1995, they began to contemplate the Internet and how they were going to keep up with this pervasive modern technology. One thing lead to another and they decided to sell Donovan & Green to an Internet company in Silicon Valley, USWeb/CKS. Although an extremely difficult decision for them, they were ready to move on and to embrace what they term "yet another new phenomenon." Today they both have different roles in USWeb/CKS. Nancye has a management role as Executive Partner Northeast Region, where she brings together strategy, creative direction, and technology. Michael focuses on the creation of environments that enhance image, communication, and brand strategy.

Their education at Parsons gave them the tools they need to succeed today. Nancye says, "Parsons was provocative, intellectually challenging, and idealistic." They saw their teachers as professionals who believed in transforming power of design. They both felt Parsons equipped them to give proper thought to issues in the environment they were hoping to affect.

"We believe in the power of design to shape our lives. Design can bridge the gap between what is possible and what people really need to lead positive and productive lives. We help our clients transform their businesses and their relationships to their customers, their employees and their communities. These are important and large assignments. We need to equip ourselves, and as educators we need to make certain we equip our students, with the discipline and experiences required to participate in the invention of this new order."

Fashion Design

DONNA KARAN

"Everything I do is a matter of the heart, body and soul. For me, designing is a personal expression of who I am— wife, mother, friend and businessperson; the many roles women everywhere are trying to balance. But, before I can be anything else, I'm a woman, with all the complications, feelings and emotions."

Born in Long Island, NY, Donna is no stranger to the fashion world. Her father was a haberdasher and her mother worked as a showroom model and as a fashion showroom representative. Even her stepfather was in the fashion industry. So, her start in her career seemed almost inevitable. In fact, she started designing by making her first collection for a fashion show in high school.

Donna attended the Parsons School of Design in New York City. Following her second year at Parsons, Donna went to work for Anne Klein as an associate designer—a job that would shape the rest of her professional life. After three years on the job and after the death of Anne Klein, Donna became Klein's successor. Louis Dell Olio, a friend from Parsons, joined her a year later and together they designed the entire Anne Klein collection. In what is said to be the fore-shadowing of the DKNY, Donna designed the Anne Klein II collection. It was the beginning of something very big for Donna.

With ten years of experience on Seventh Avenue, Donna decided it was time to go out on her own. With the support of her family, friends and business partners, Donna "set up shop in her living room," learning as she went along.

Her educational experience at Parsons was very important to her career. Although she graduated many years ago, she still spends as much time as possible today at her alma mater where she lectures and critiques students' work. She believes "it's so important to give back." Donna also sits on Parsons's Board of Governors and on the Board of Trustees of the Martha Graham Center of Contemporary Dance.

Donna Karan credits her feminine instincts for the success of her company, founded with her husband Stephen Weiss in 1984. "That I am a woman makes me want to nurture others, fulfill needs and solve problems." This is the basis for forming DKNY and it is the driving force behind what Donna sees as her mission in designing clothes for men and women. She places great emphasis on designing from "head-to-toe."

TOP & BELOW
Donna Karan Collection, 1999
ARTIST PHOTO
Harry Heleotis

REBECCA KAUFMAN

"I consider myself lucky to have been born a designer—to enjoy striving for aesthetic perfection. Success lies in an end result that reaches people, serves a purpose or function, and clothes the body beautifully. My advice to perspective students is to attempt to learn and discover as much as possible. If the natural urge is to be a part of design in life, then DO! The design field is so rewarding."

Rebecca is a 1990 graduate of Otis College of Art and Design, where she had the highest grade point average of any fashion design student since the program's inception in 1980. She was named the best fashion illustrator by the Professional Critics Panel, won a professional excellence award from the Textile Association of Los Angeles, and won first, second and third place in design competitions for Nike Men's Shoe Division.

As the Senior Designer at Nike she now designs, coordinates and sketches five full collections a year—researching and selecting seasonal fabrics and trims, providing final approval for fabric color, print and production, following the complete developmental cycle through to retail, and taking on many other responsibilities. Her personal area of work is tennis apparel and women's technical apparel.

Rebecca has been with Nike for seven years and considers herself lucky to encounter such incredible talent in one place. Regardless of whether she is working with designers, production teams, or image consultants, all aspects of all teams are superior. She says that Nike is dedicated to developing and

designing top quality, technologically advanced footwear and apparel. It is her job to "find the equation that will enhance the athletic performance of the body, and make it look stunning, modern and innovative at the same time."

Rebecca's time at Otis was extremely meaningful to her. She feels the professionalism of the fashion design department is very important to aspiring graduates. She found her education inspiring, personable, nurturing, and, most important, demanding. She feels Otis takes extra care to provide "real world" design critics from various backgrounds who challenge the students to achieve all they can.

TOP, ABOVE & LEFT
Nike tennis apparel, 1999
Photos courtesy of Nike

HILARY BROUGHER

TOP
Terumi Matthews in
The Sticky Fingers of Time

ABOVE
Hilary Brougher on film set

RIGHT
Promotion for
The Sticky Fingers of Time

ARTIST PHOTO
Ethan Mass

Hilary Brougher sees her career in three distinct phases. Her interest in filmmaking developed quite early, for she began making her own Super-8 films at age 14. Hilary calls this her "home movie" phase—the time spent messing around on her own, shooting her friends and her daily life. She values this time, because it gave her "a chance to experiment and fall in love with the medium without too much pressure to conform."

Hilary's second phase was "film school." She attended the School of Visual Arts (SVA) in New York City and received her BFA in 1990. To her, this time was essential "for learning how to work with people, to access equipment and ideas, and to continue the experimentation I began on my own." It was also a time to make friends and connections; she still works with people she met at SVA ten years ago.

Then came "real life" after graduation. Hilary worked with various film production companies in New York and "learned how films are really put together (something you can glimpse in school but can't really understand until you do it)." Again, she expanded her contact and group of peers, many of whom she works with today.

During this time, she also wrote and directed her first feature film "The Sticky Fingers of Time", which was completed in 1997 (with cinematography by her classmate Ethan Mass). The film has since traveled to more than 150 international film festivals and had a small theatrical release through Strand Releasing. New York film critics have said "Brougher's first feature is a crisply executed, deeply engrossing time-travel yarn that packs more ideas into 81 minutes than some movies do in three hours." "Brougher has set up a cinematic baklava, which successfully layers an intimate human story with sci-fi and mystery devises."

GOOD MACHINE PRESENTS
THE STICKY FINGERS OF TIME
A FILM BY HILARY BROUGHER

OFFICIAL SELECTION
1997 VENICE INTERNATIONAL
FILM FESTIVAL · OFICINA

OFFICIAL SELECTION
1997 TORONTO INTERNATIONAL
FILM FESTIVAL

OFFICIAL SELECTION
1998 ROTTERDAM INTERNATIONAL
FILM FESTIVAL

HTTP://WWW.ESCAPE.COM/~STICKY

"Keep your projects do-able—don't go broke making your thesis film. And know that you have to do the "real world" part of training as well. Be prepared to work for little or no money doing thankless jobs at first. But make friends and learn!"

Film and Video

DOUG HALL

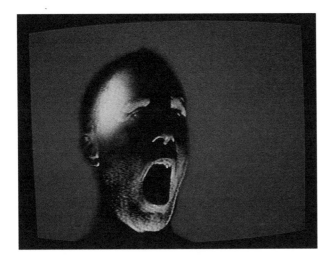

and installation pieces that built his reputation in the 30 years since he graduated from MICA.

Doug Hall has received considerable recognition for his work, including fellowships from the Guggenheim Museum, the Fulbright and the Rockefeller Foundations, and the National Endowment for the Arts. His work has appeared in over 30 solo exhibitions and is in the permanent collections of the Whitney Museum of American Art and the Museum of Modern Art, among others. Doug has been a faculty member at the San Francisco Art Institute since 1981.

He says that in art college "everything opened up for me— I could explore things I couldn't in a standard academic setting. I gained a full visual vocabulary and came in contact with some very smart people." Doug sees the future as full of new possibilities because video has become so ubiquitous; video equipment is cheaper now, and TV has made us comfortable with the medium.

TOP
The Terrible Uncertainty of the Thing Described, installation detail, 1987

LEFT
The Victims' Regret, video installation detail, 1984

BELOW RIGHT
The Plains of San Agustin, video installation, 1986

"Art is a way to position yourself in the world."

Doug Hall prefers to call himself a "media artist," feeling this is a broad enough label that he can't be pigeon-holed into any one category. More specifically, no matter what medium he works in, he sees himself as an "imagist." The constant theme of his work is concern with how we react to the images we encounter and how we gather meaning from the world around us. Doug feels particularly strongly about the individual's diminishing power in the face of the overwhelming power of electronic and broadcast media.

Doug received an undergraduate degree in Anthropology and Art History from Harvard University in 1966. While there, he did some video and performance work, and decided that he should pursue his art interest on a full-time basis. He enrolled in the graduate sculpture program at the Maryland Institute, College of Art (MICA), but soon gravitated back towards video, installation, and performance work. And while he is now turning towards photography in a substantial way, it is his video

Fine Arts

TIM ROLLINS AND K.O.S.

"John Dewey said it best. 'Education is a total work of art.'
For me, being a teacher is my work of art."

TOP
**Animal Farm—
Jesse Helms,**
1988

RIGHT
**Invisible Man
(after Ralph Ellison),**
1999

BELOW
**Amerika—The
Stoker (after Franz
Kafka),** 1990

PHOTO OF
TIM ROLLINS
AND K.O.S
Robert Morris

Tim Rollins was born and raised in Maine. He attended two years of University in Maine, before transferring to the School of Visual Arts (SVA) in New York, where he received his BFA in 1978. He then got a teaching certificate from New York University in 1980. During the early '80s he also joined Group Material (see profile of Doug Ashford and Group Material, page 52).

In 1982 Tim became an art teacher in Intermediate School 52 in the South Bronx and was asked to set up an art program for "at risk" youth. Shortly after, in response to this request, he gathered his students and formed K.O.S. (Kids of Survival). An NEA grant in 1984 allowed K.O.S. to get space of their own and to found the Art and Knowledge Workshop, Inc. Since then, Art and Knowledge has become a national organization, with operations in Memphis, San Francisco and throughout New York City.

Tim felt his students had been written off by society and their creative intelligence had been ignored. They had visual talent, however, and he wanted to use art as a vehicle to access other school subjects as well. Art classes became a way to motivate and empower these students and to show that disadvantaged youth were capable of producing art that has an impact. And it was also a way to question the traditions and hierarchy of the art world. The art produced by Tim Rollins and K.O.S is often political in nature and always a collaborative, group effort. The students gain an appreciation of the workings of the art world, while the art world has some of its cherished assumptions turned upside-down.

Tim attributes his rewarding career to chance; he was reading an article on art and philosophy by Joseph Kosuth, learned he was a faculty member at SVA, and decided then and there to transfer. He says, "SVA gave me the opportunity to study with dozens of extraordinary artists, critics and scholars who all generously encouraged what has become my life's work."

DOUG AND MIKE STARN

Identical twin brothers, Mike and Doug were born in New Jersey in 1961. Taking photographs was an early interest for both of them—they started at age 13. Eventually, they both graduated from The School of the Museum of Fine Arts in Boston. They managed to excel through the four-year program in three years and in their final year won two of the Museum School's competitive Fifth Year Traveling Scholarships which facilitated their first major public installation.

Much of their early work was photographs Scotch-taped together and push-pinned directly into the wall. The Starns now define themselves as fine artists working in photography, computer, sculpture and film/video. After graduation, success followed quickly with solo shows in galleries and museums in New York City and Boston and San Francisco. Their work was in the Whitney Biennial in 1987 and the subject of a monograph published by Harry N. Abrams in 1990.

They are at their studio 8 hours a day, five days a week. Much of their time is devoted to the business aspect of what they do with the balance dedicated to conceptualizing artworks or the practical matters of how to create them for exhibition. Their tasks are not always easy and they constantly experiment with new techniques and processes. Recently, they were faced with the challenge of how to evenly distribute the weight in a steel sculpture that would spin in two directions simultaneously while lit internally with 3,000 watts of halogen lamps.

Current new projects include two photographic series called "Blot Out the Sun" and "Attracted to Light," along with a new video sculpture and a film project with actor Dennis Hopper.

Both brothers agree that the School of the Museum of Fine Arts (SMFA) was the "perfect" school for them. It provided an environment which allowed them to develop their creativity at their own pace and to follow their own interests wherever that took them. They feel the school encourages creativity over achieving a certain "grade." Doug and Mike were able to "look into themselves for what they needed to express and how they wanted to communicate that expression" without feeling pressured by traditional departmental limitations.

"It is our hope that fine art will continue to provide a soul and a consciousness and a depth and a mirror to our culture, as it always has. Art speaks from within individuals to society and to the future."

Fine Arts

JASON DODGE

"Being interesting is far more important than making interesting work."

After high school, Jason went to community college for a year and then transferred to Maryland Institute, College of Art (MICA) in Baltimore. He received his BFA from MICA in 1992, and while there studied abroad in Malawi, Africa, and Florence, Italy. He then lived in Minnesota for two years, graduated from Yale University's MFA program, and moved to New York City in 1996.

Since then he has been in group exhibitions in Sweden, Japan and New York, and in solo exhibitions in Basel, Tokyo, and New York. Only two years after graduation, Jason was named one of the top ten artists of 1998 by "Artforum" magazine and he received favorable reviews in "The New Yorker" and the "New York Times". His work is now in the permanent collection of the Guggenheim Museum in New York.

Although Jason's degree from MICA reads "BFA in Painting" he developed a strong interest in sculpture towards the end of his undergraduate studies. His work now consists of installations of assembled and invented objects. Jason calls his work "a merging of fiction and design—a narration through style." Mingling icons of fashion, graphic design, industrial design, film, and pop music, he seeks to raise questions about corporate image-making and universal culture.

For Jason, his education at Maryland provided "valuable flexibility; a place with few limitations in terms of work content, where I could work with all kinds of people and interests."

TOP
Chairs, 1999–2000

ABOVE
Plants, 1999–2000

LEFT
Storage, 1997–1998

PHOTOS
Casey Kaplan

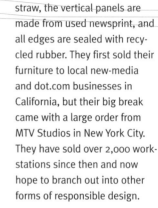

EREZ STEINBERG & GIA SULLO

Erez was born and raised in Israel, and then came to the United States in 1984. After a few years in different colleges in San Francisco, he enrolled in California College of Arts & Crafts (CCAC), where he received his BFA in Industrial Design in 1991. Shortly after graduation he and his wife Gia Sullo (a graphic design graduate of CCAC), formed their own company, Studio eg. After a moment of inspiration while digging through a pile of garbage in the industrial neighborhood where they live, the two designers proceeded to successfully carve out a niche for themselves in the $10 billion office furniture market.

Studio eg produces EcoWork, a full line of office workstations made from 100% recovered and recycled materials. The legs are recycled carpet tubes, tabletops are made from leftover wheat-straw, the vertical panels are made from used newsprint, and all edges are sealed with recycled rubber. They first sold their furniture to local new-media and dot.com businesses in California, but their big break came with a large order from MTV Studios in New York City. They have sold over 2,000 workstations since then and now hope to branch out into other forms of responsible design.

"Before we began, we had to ask ourselves serious questions," Steinberg said. "Do we have the right to exist? Does the world need another desk? Will this product contribute to society?" Eventually, their commitment to "green" materials and processes provided the answers to those questions, and the result is the colorful, environmentally friendly furniture they now market.

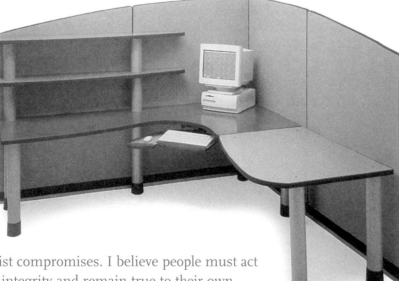

"I resist compromises. I believe people must act with integrity and remain true to their own values. You have to do what you believe in and be willing to pay the price along the way."

TOP & LEFT
Ecowork,
office furniture
system

PHOTOS
Tony Stromberg

KAREN SEPANSKI

"I know that I want to continue to grow and evolve. Whether this impacts society or is merely a blip on the radar screen of the planet is not of much concern to me. If there are those who see my work as important and as a contribution, I am appreciative."

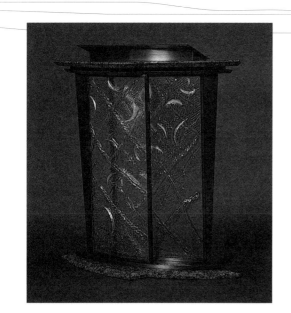

TOP & ABOVE
Glass/Metal Pulpit,
1999
PHOTOS
Charles Cloud III

As a self-described "lifelong learner," Karen Sepanski has had a varied career spanning over 20 years. She has a BFA in ceramics, a MA in Art Education, and K-12 art teacher certification. An alumnus of the Center for Creative Studies (CCS) in Detroit, Karen is known for, among other things, her talent in glass. She began with the basics of glass blowing and experimentation with other glass processes. After graduation she apprenticed in a traditional stained glass studio while pursuing her own aesthetic and artistic development. As she says, she was fortunate to have been chosen for a significant public arts commission—a skylight—that helped launch her career and her own design studio in Detroit.

Early in her career, Karen made architectural bas-relief panels and colorful bent and fused glass collages, similar to paintings. She then began to produce and market an array of functional and decorative platters, bowls, dinnerware and lighting. Today she travels regularly to trade shows and art fairs, as well as exhibiting her work in galleries.

In addition to a line of houseware items, Karen worked on several large architectural commissions including lighting for office buildings, wall dividers for restaurants, and glass murals for nightclubs and theaters. Currently, Karen is designing a baptismal font, pulpit and altar for a Lutheran Church in Bloomfield Hills, Michigan, near Detroit. She is collaborating with a metalsmith and a stonemason on the project.

When asked about her educational experience and how it helped her prepare for her career in glass, Karen wasn't reserved in her response. She credits her broad visual education with allowing her to find the tools necessary to become an "maker of objects." She isn't sure whether it was the influence of her contemporary Chinese history, her sixth grade teacher, or her biology teacher who excused her from class to design the holiday bulletin board, that gave her the inspiration to find her passion in art. What she is sure of is that she is indebted to all of her teachers for the challenges they presented her and for the realization that no single experience or adventure was the identifiable source of her passion to be a "lifelong learner" of the arts. Each experience was a part of the whole.

MALCOLM GREAR

"I am a lucky man. Not by design, but through design, I have gained a life of friendships, respectful affection, delightful collaboration—all born of my work, which in itself, in its daily texture and visual diversity, brings pleasure to my soul. I know that I will never reach complete satisfaction in my work, I am still on the open sea, but there is nothing that I would rather do than design."

Born in rural Kentucky, Malcolm Grear was eleven before electricity was installed in his neighborhood. He says "precious little was wasted" back then and that most of his playthings were home made. After a four-year stint in the Navy, Malcolm attended the Art of Academy of Cincinnati. He credits his experience at the Art Academy with helping him see beyond two dimensions and broadening his sense of materials. He learned early to avoid thinking that each visual art had its own exclusive language. "Visual dialect or idiom may vary, but there is unity across diverse forms of art."

While in college he served as a teaching assistant in both the metal shop and photography lab. He says his teachers thought of him as a sculptor and he assumed they thought he was a photographer. Whatever his teachers thought he was going to do in the art world, Malcolm knew he wanted to be a graphic designer. He was confident that he could adapt his chosen profession to what he wanted to do, just as he had with the objects of his childhood.

Shortly after graduating from the Art Academy he took a teaching position at the Rhode Island School of Design from which he recently retired. At the same time he secured his first design commission. This facilitated the formation of Malcolm Grear Designs (MGD) in 1960.

Committed to innovation—initially within traditional vehicles of communication such as corporate logos, books, catalogues, and signs—MGD soon applied its talents to presentations of sophisticated information in textbooks, technology, exhibitions, and financial institutions.

From his simple rearing in rural Kentucky, Malcolm has come to work on the same level as scholars and professionals in many arenas. In his 1994 book "Inside/Outside," he described his goals as: "To present values as well as facts, to discover meaning, to organize information, to integrate the verbal and the numerical with the pictorial and sculptural, to create something fresh but enduring, to combine strength with elegance."

TOP
Pictogram,
1996 Olympic Games

RIGHT
Olympic Torch,
1996 Olympic Games

LEFT
Pictogram Series,
1996 Olympic Games

ARTIST PHOTO
Ron Carraher

Quilt of leaves etched on gold-plated band

22 aluminum reeds, one for each of the modern Olympic Games

Each host city etched in a gold-plated band

Propane fuel tank reflective of Greek and Southern architecture

REGINA RODRIGUES

"Graphic designers must possess a high level of perception and human understanding. And they must always remember that they are not creating something for themselves. There will always be a future for Graphic Designers as long as humankind exists on this planet, because people will always need to communicate in one form or another."

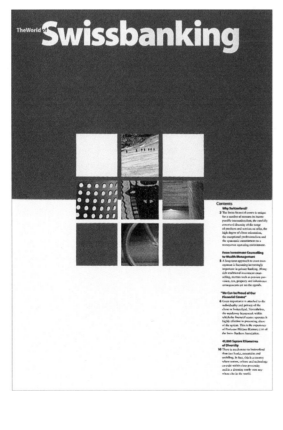

Although born in Cleveland, Ohio, Regina Rodrigues grew up in Rio de Janeiro. She studied business administration in Brazil before returning to the United States to attend the Corcoran College of Art and Design, where she received her BFA in Graphic Design. She also did postgraduate work at the Basel School of Design in Switzerland. Regina became an assistant Art Director at a firm in Washington, DC, following her graduation and then went on to freelance design work. From 1991 to 1993 she taught Graphic Design at the Corcoran and other schools in Washington, DC. She then returned to Switzerland to work as a Senior Graphic Designer at Gottschalk & Ash and also worked on a special book project, "Artist Book: Structure, Content, Sequence."

Regina defines Graphic Design as something that mutates and expands daily. It is a way of living, thinking and existing. She says, "you have to love it, otherwise do not even bother. It is not a 9–5 occupation, it is something you live and breathe even when you are in the super market. Graphic Designers must constantly be looking for solutions and be able to register all the visual and verbal material they encounter in everyday life." She believes her work helps people define their communications needs—whether a product, corporate identity or things as simple a color, texture, shapes and forms.

Illustration

"My chosen discipline, Illustration, is always evolving as our society evolves and our planet gets smaller. We will always have the need to conceptualize, to present ideas to each other, and to stimulate intellect and interest."

EZRA TUCKER

TOP
Bedouin Favorites,
1995

ABOVE
**Return of the
Titans,** 1995

Ezra Tucker was fascinated since childhood with exotic lands, mythologies, legends and tales of adventure. When he had to chose between archeology and art as a career, art won when he realized that his wide-ranging interests, plus a sense of adventure, could all be creatively achieved through painting.

A graduate of Memphis College of Art in Tennessee, his award-winning work has been exhibited throughout the United States. Ezra's imaginative compositions aptly demonstrate his unique point of view and versatile talent. He describes his style as "Nouveau Victorian Realism," where people, animals and landscapes are realistically depicted in fantastic settings reminiscent of Victorian period painters. He says he often starts a project by saying "Can you imagine.....?"

Ezra's career as a commercial illustrator hinges on continuous problem solving. His clients use his communication skills and artistic abilities to sell their products and to communicate their ideas or specific points-of-view to the public. He finds his work extremely challenging and stimulating. His client base is international and varied, ranging from individuals to giant corporations.

"I often reflect on the scope of my interest and the academic requirements during my college career," says Ezra. It was his education at Memphis that prepared him for his career as an Illustrator and gave him the self-discipline necessary to excel. College encouraged him to reach as far as he wished and always to approach every challenge with creative thinking.

Industrial Design and Product Design

ROBERT MEURER

"Good design can humanize technology, and as designers we in one form or another determine its application. The inverse is equally important in developing products that utilize both socially and environmentally responsible processes and materials as well as providing for an end of the life plan: i.e., sustainable use, recycling, reclamation. In keeping pace with technology, the future potential of design and its benefits hold only as much a we have to offer, no more, no less."

A 1992 graduate of the Milwaukee Institute of Art & Design, Robert Meurer has a proven track record of accomplishments in both the domestic and global design markets. His career has ranged from being a research and development assistant at Buell Motorcycles while in college, to being a staff designer at Johnson Controls, to his current position as a Senior Industrial Designer for General Electric Medical Systems.

Practicing Industrial Design within the medical industry is very rewarding, yet challenging for Robert. He is respectful of the unique relationship between the product and the patient. In addition to maintaining standards of ergonomics, styling, manufacturing and serviceability, he now has to cope with the complex application of technology. For him, the most important criteria for the successful design of a medical appliance are simple—relieving patient anxiety and discomfort, while providing a product that is easy and efficient to use. This ultimately helps ensure a higher level of patient care and recovery.

Robert believes that design is rapidly changing, regardless of industry or field. As a designer, he believes he must be able to grow, adapt, and above all embrace change. He says, "I'd like to think there is no such thing as a complacent designer." He strongly believes that commitment and education have given him the solid foundation for what continues to be a constant learning process.

TOP
EZ-EM Biopsy Gun, sketch detail, 1996

RIGHT
Spinal Injury Patient Cart, 1992

Industrial Design and Product Design

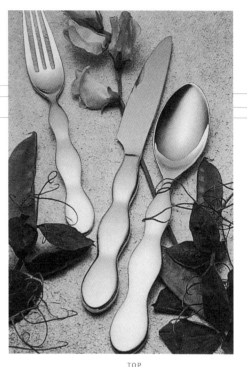

FREDERIC SPECTOR

A 1984 graduate of the University of the Arts, Frederic Spector currently runs his own design firm, Frederic Spector Design Studios, in Providence, Rhode Island. In addition, Frederic is an adjunct faculty member at the Rhode Island School of Design (RISD) where he teaches furniture and lighting design. RISD is also where he completed his Masters degree in Industrial Design in 1988.

Since graduating college, Frederic has had many job opportunities that have shaped his career in the design field. He worked as a furniture craftsman, as senior designer for an interior/industrial design firm, and as a designer for a residential lighting company. In his current position, he heads his own design firm specializing in furniture, lighting, flatware, dinner- ware, and glassware design for clients throughout the country. His designs are licensed to well-known manufacturers in return for royalties or flat fees. Frederic says it is critical that the designer be aware of fast-moving trends and technology, as well as materials and fabrication techniques, in addition to the obvious aesthetic concerns.

Frederic says his education provided him with a foundation of skills and hands-on experience that allows him to think and create the way he does today. He felt better prepared to meet his client's needs by first learning the basics of how furniture and other objects are made. Equally important, Frederic believes the ties to his instructors and advisors served to bolster his confidence in his work. His undergraduate education at the University of the Arts combined with work and life experiences prepared him well for the rigors of postgraduate study. At RISD he was challenged to develop his conceptual design thinking further and to consider design in new dimensions: its relationship to industry and production needs as well as to the end-user.

TOP
Pyramid Lamp, Thos. Moser Cabinetmakers

ABOVE
Skal Flatware, DANSK International Design Ltd.

LEFT
Bed, Bassett Furniture Industries

"As society enters the 21st century, lifestyles will demand new design to accommodate change in the way people work and live. Computer technology is playing a big role in the design process and will continue to be more important in the future."

LAURA BOVA

TOP
The Jerome Schottenstein Center Novelty Store, 1999

BELOW
Children's Hospital, Close to Home Health Care Center, 1999

ARTIST PHOTO
Leslee Kass

Laura Bova graduated in 1994 with a BFA degree from the Columbus College of Arts and Design (CCAD). Since then she has held positions with several design firms before landing her current job a few years ago with Moody/Nolan Ltd., Inc as an interior designer.

She characterizes her position as one full of variety and challenges, where she is constantly learning—whether it is about the newest finishes, lighting, furniture products or the best construction method to build a display case. She works on everything from renovating older buildings to designing university libraries, bank branches, corporate offices, retail spaces, hospital cancer wards, college dormitories, assisted living facilities and sports arenas.

"In the future, 3-D computer-generated images and 'fly throughs' of interior spaces will continue to grow as a design presentation tool. Designers who develop this skill can look forward to many employment opportunities."

Through it all she acknowledges the need to work as a member of a collaborative team of professionals. The team may include interior designers, architects, CAD technicians, electrical and mechanical engineers and a host of others. She is now involved in projects from the schematic design phase to final construction and installation, including attending client meetings and maintaining communication with all parties for the duration of the design project. She sees verbal and written communication, technical knowledge, organizational skills, time management and creativity as essential skills for doing her job well.

During her college education Laura learned to think and communicate visually. Her training in color, painting, and drawing, prepared her for her career today. Laura also gives credit to her teachers not only because of what they taught her about her discipline, but also because they worked in the field and brought real life experiences to the classroom. She also advocates working if possible while in school, part time, to gain experience and to network with those in your chosen field.

VALERIE SCHMEIDER

tural elements that either exist or that she helps to develop. By "environment" she means all the elements that make up the space, the volume, the shape, the color and materials, the lighting, the textures, the built-in and movable furnishings and the technology. And always, she has to be mindful of the need to create these environments within her clients' goals, budgets, time frames.

A graduate of the Kendall College of Art and Design in 1986, Valerie followed a natural path to becoming the owner and principal of VIA Design, Inc., in Grand Rapids, Michigan. Valerie was born into a family deeply rooted in the business of design. Her parents owned a furniture store in the small town in which she grew up and her mother was an interior designer as well. It was in her parents' store that Valerie learned everything from drapery fabrication to sales.

In speaking of her career, Valerie believes that interior designers are responsible for creating total environments that meet the various needs of clients. She works within the architec-

Her education at Kendall exposed Valerie to all aspects of the design profession, including aesthetics, historical references, environmental concerns, professional practices and general design concerns. The exposure to these elements allowed Valerie to enter her chosen profession already possessing a good working knowledge of interior design and how the industry works. Her own innate artistic ability was enhanced and challenged in new applications at school. And, by participating in Kendall's "co-op" work program, she was able to acquire her first design position immediately following graduation.

TOP
Master Bath, private residence, 1999

LEFT
Great Room, private residence, 1999

ARTIST PHOTO
Chuck Heiney

"The profession of interior design is growing and changing as new products and new materials offer new solutions to society's needs. The use of computers in the industry has broadened the possibilities and increased productivity. It is a very exciting time to consider a career in interior design."

ANN KING LAGOS

"People always remember when they receive their first piece of sparkling jewels from someone who adores them. It is also a form of personal expression that changes and grows every day. People wear jewelry not only to remember a cherished moment, but also to say something about themselves to the outside world. The future of jewelry is both as changing and as certain as it was in the past—and it will always be with us."

A graduate of the University of the Arts (UArts) in Philadelphia, in 1976, Ann King Lagos earned her BFA degree in jewelry and metalsmithing. After graduation, she set out to open her own design firm known as Ann King Designs. Her designs were reminiscent of architecture and nature—things she had been influenced by from her youth. In 1984 Ann met another young jewelry designer named Steven Lagos. They married in 1987 and together merged their two businesses into what is now known as the House of Lagos. The merger, both personal and professional is a great success, and their company has become one of the most successful designer jewelry brands in the country.

Ann sees her creations as being about passion and aesthetics on every level. However, although jewelry design is her chosen career, she also enjoys creating window displays for the retail store, or working on a charity event's invitation, or painting furniture for her daughter's room; Ann sees all things creatively. The House of Lagos has won numerous awards for their unique designs reflecting the seasons, nature and the world around them. Their flagship store is located in the heart of Philadelphia and they have smaller boutiques in New York, Beverly Hills, and Las Vegas.

When asked about her education, Ann feels strongly that her time at art school was what prepared her for her career. Specifically, she was encouraged to see many sides of things, to be open to new ideas and to be able to find and use the inspiration all around her. She knows that it was at school where she learned the technical skills and furthered her knowledge and appreciation for metals and jewelry, but she came away with more than the basic training. She feels her educational experience provided her with a genuine, rarefied creative environment in which to learn. She also very much enjoys the urban life that Philadelphia offers and she loves the city's neighborly atmosphere and rich history.

TOP
Lagos Caviar™ Suite

ABOVE LEFT
**Lagos Signature
Heart Pendants**

RIGHT
**Lagos Marquee
Collection Bracelet
and Ring**

Multi-Media and New Media

ERIC EATON

Eric Eaton is the son of a circus strongman and aerialist who settled in Vermont in the mid 1960s. He moved to New York in the late 1980s to purse a career in theater and music, but returned home disliking big city life. After a few failed attempts at making a career as an exhibit builder and sign painter, Eric moved to Portland, Maine to study graphic design at the Maine College of Art (MECA). After graduation, he moved to San Francisco to work for Wired Digital, a division of Wired Magazine, to help develop a suite of online products— Webmonkey, Wired News and HotBot. In 1999 he returned to Portland, Maine, but retains his position as Design Director for Wired Digital, telecommuting from his home.

Eric's work in the computer and media field is driven by typography, language, and the systems and symbols that people encounter in everyday life. He feels that when taken as a whole they tell a story about our culture and ourselves. He is fascinated with the narrative process and tries to design things that are engaging and entertaining, as well as serving a useful purpose. He sees himself as both a designer and a storyteller.

MECA provided Eric with a rigorous education in design and the chance to synthesize the collective knowledge of a hundred talented people. Although his specialized field of Interactive Media was virtually unknown at that time, it was apparent to him that the field of graphic design was about to move into the realm of the unfamiliar. His education prepared him to "think beyond familiar idioms" and to participate in what "amounted to a design revolution."

Eric encourages students not to become preoccupied with their careers while in school. He believes that students should take advantage of the "insulation from the industry" and allow themselves the time to hone their visual and intellectual skills. He sees one's uniqueness and individuality as the key to a successful career.

TOP & LEFT webpages for **wired.com,** 1998

BELOW **netsurfcentral.com** promotional design, 1996

"I expect the field of Interactive Design and Multimedia will become increasingly more important in the future. As information becomes the commodity of the global community, greater demands will be placed on designers. We will need to extend the role of designers to include writers, engineers and artists. Collectively, such people will create a much more interesting and sustainable creative environment."

JIM OCKULY

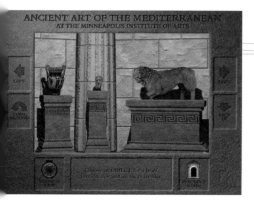

TOP
Omegaville,
1998

ABOVE
Ancient Art of the Mediterranean,
Minneapolis
Institute of Art, 1995

RIGHT
Obstacle Course,
1999

The youngest of seven children, Jim Ockuly was born in Saint Paul, Minnesota. He has had an accomplished and interesting life following his graduation from Minneapolis College of Art and Design (MCAD) in 1983. Jim traveled to Berlin to write and paint in 1984, received a residency at P.S. 1 in New York through the Minnesota State Arts Board in 1986, was commissioned by the Walker Art Center to create a temporary mural in 1988, and since 1991 has worked full time at the Minneapolis Institute of Art's Interactive Media Group.

Jim's "day job" is as a multi-media producer, but he is also an artist who makes and shows his art outside of the context of his job—personal projects

that he found himself compelled to do, whether they supported him financially or not. These parallel activities (his own art and his art job) have contributed to each other in ways Jim never thought possible. He'll "stumble upon a discovery in one realm and be able to transfer it to the other." He has even found that human interaction as part of his museum work has remedied the isolation of his own studio work.

As a multimedia producer Jim is currently working on an interactive program about the collection of Modernist design work for the museum and on a computer-based game called the "Obstacle Course" for himself.

Jim describes himself as a horrible student before going to art school. "It's not that I was stupid, but I just didn't work well in that traditional educational system." College changed everything—his creativity was recognized and encouraged; his ideas and his surroundings finally had something in common. As Jim puts it, "the emphasis on developing one's own sense of looking at things and on applying critical thinking to all forms of representation and expression—especially one's own—prepared me for all that was to come."

"It's funny—people may not say that artists are important or necessary, but when someone says the right thing at the right moment in just the right way and it sheds light on the world in such a way that it gets everyone out of a jam or reminds them why we're here or stimulates a whole new way of thinking, they'll call that person an artist. And, even though you or I may never contribute that earth-shattering comment or image or idea, it's kind of fun to be constantly preparing to do just that."

Multi-Media and New Media

BEN STOKES

"Ten years ago we were a relatively unique company—now there are hundreds like us. We are seeing rapid generational changes, brought about by cheaper and easier access to the necessary equipment."

TOP
Still from **Helter Skelter '97**

BELOW
Stills from **DJ Asylum,** The Orb,
Island Records UK, 1997

Ben Stokes was born in 1965 and raised in Minneapolis, Minnesota. He was brought up in a musical family—his father is an experimental composer who writes for traditional and non traditional orchestras and his mother is a flutist for the St. Paul Chamber orchestra—and is always involved in music himself. Perhaps it is natural that his visual and musical talents are now so closely aligned. Ben is co-founder and a director of a multi-media video and TV production company called H-GUN Labs, headquartered in San Francisco.

Ben arrived in Chicago in 1984 to attend the School of the Art Institute of Chicago (SAIC) from which he graduated. While studying film, sound, animation and video at SAIC, he began to explore the world of music and film outside of school. He formed a band with fellow art students called UNGH! and began to show his student films at local venues. Eventually, using school equipment, they merged these two interests by creating two music videos for Ministry. Thus H-GUN was born (the name is taken from UNGH! by scrambling the letters).

Working in a small firm, Ben says he does everything—he is a sound technician, an editor, an artist, and a director all at the same time. Although he considers himself a fine artist at heart, Ben and his colleagues are certainly successful commercial artists in every sense. H-GUN now produces ads, videos and TV spots for the Sci-Fi Channel, Comedy Central, and the Cartoon Network, among others. In 1998, his firm's work was honored at the Broadcast Design Awards with 2 gold, 3 silver, and 6 bronze medals.

Ben says he got a lot out of his education because he put a lot into it. Good people and equipment are available, to be sure, but students have to bring their own motivation and initiative to the process as well. He sees college as a time to push yourself to do things you might not otherwise do.

RIGO ØØ

TOP
Innercity Home, 1995
Photo by Diego Diaz

ABOVE
Birds and Cars, 1997
Photo by Kenny Trice

RIGHT
One Tree, 1995
Photo by Kenny Trice

"Through putting art directly in public space,
I remain engaged as a citizen and an artist in the
life of the city.

Rigo ØØ was born on Madeira Island, Portugal in 1966. He came to San Francisco, California in 1986 to begin his studies at the San Francisco Art Institute (SFAI) on a scholarship. He completed his BFA in 1991 and went on to Stanford University where he earned his MFA in 1997. Rigo ØØ (last year he was Rigo 99, and the year before,

Rigo 98) has devoted much of his time working with youth. From 1992 to 1994 he worked at the International Studies Academy, a San Francisco public high school. He currently conducts several workshops specifically designed for inner city youth, works with a group of students from San Francisco's magnet high school, School of the Arts, and also teaches at SFAI.

When asked to discuss his career, Rigo ØØ says he stays very busy making as much art as he can and stays engaged with the audiences partial to his work. He divides his time between studio work—painting, drawing, thinking, and building—and the "street/public" work he does that is site-specific for a particular constituency or for a particular location. His work—large scale paintings—can be seen on the sides of buildings throughout San Francisco.

Rigo ØØ has done various residencies abroad as well, which have had tremendous impact on his life. He is working on a series of several large canvases depicting urban scenes in Taiwan where he lived for two years.

His work will be exhibited this year in a solo exhibition at the Gallery Paule Anglim in San Francisco. His future projects include a public art project including sculpture and the use of mosaic stone for his hometown, Madeira Island.

Rigo ØØ says his education often consisted of "thinking out loud" in front of his peers and recognizing the need to erase any formal prejudices associated with a particular medium. In other words, he was taught to consider the unique situation, to consider what he wanted to achieve artistically, and then to decide which medium and which approach would be most effective for that situation. Rigo ØØ says his time in college was both a scary and exhilarating process all at the same time. What more could a student ask for?

DOUG ASHFORD AND GROUP MATERIAL

"I hope that everybody thinks about what is valuable. How somethings are held in one's mind to be above other things is a great ongoing question. Those discussions are important to have on a public level, as well as in museums and among strangers. The objects we make, or the collections we arrange, can question the established spaces that surround us."

Doug Ashford graduated from the Cooper Union, School of Art, with a BFA in 1981. He has been an influential artist, teacher, writer, and activist ever since. He currently teaches at Cooper Union and is the Director of the MFA in Visual Arts Program at Vermont College. He says "teaching has always been as important as my artistic work." Although he is probably best known for his collaboration with Group Material, he also exhibits and lectures on a regular basis in academies and museums around the world.

Group Material was formed in 1979 as an eclectic gathering of 15 artists and non-artist friends in New York City. Their initial motivation was to question the existing structure of the art world—to investigate what is art, who is it for, and how is it presented. Their manifesto was "We invite everyone to question the entire culture we have taken for granted."

Group Material started in a community-based, grassroots manner, by renting an empty storefront on the Lower East Side of Manhattan. An early, acclaimed exhibition asked neighbors of the storefront to donate objects to display which "might not usually find their way into an art gallery; the things you find personally beautiful." As they became better known and bolder, they exhibited their works in both traditional settings—museums, art centers, and arts festivals—and in

unusual sites—bus shelters, magazine inserts, and even shopping bags.

After its first year, Group Material reducing itself to a core of four people: Ashford, Julie Ault, Mundy McLaughlin, and Tim Rollins. In the mid-80s, McLaughlin and Rollins left and Felix Gonzalez-Torres joined. Through 1997, when the group dissolved, they produced over 50 exhibitions and public projects, as well as numerous publications. For their last two projects, Ashford and Ault were joined by Thomas Eggerer and Joochen Klein.

Critic Jan Avgikos wrote "the chapter (that Group Material) wrote on the theory and practice of contemporary art has shaped our common history, and will be interpreted and debated for decades to come." Indeed, Group Material has changed the way many people now conceive of how art is valued by our society.

TOP
Democracy Wall,
1984

BELOW
**Dia Art Foundation
Installation,** 1989

VINCENT DESIDERIO

Born in Philadelphia in 1955, Vincent received his Bachelor of Arts from Haverford College and then went to Italy for a year where he enrolled in the Academia di Belle Arti in Florence. In 1983, after returning to the United States, he completed a four-year Certificate from the Pennsylvania Academy of Fine Arts. While at the Academy he was awarded the Cresson Traveling Scholarship, which enable him to return to Europe for further study. In 1996, Vincent became the first North American artist to receive the Foundation Prince Pierre de Monaco's Grand Prize.

Vincent, in addition to painting, is currently a teacher at the New York Academy of Art, the Pennsylvania Academy of Fine Arts, and periodically at the School of Visual Arts, also in New York.

For a number of years now, Vincent has focused his attention as a painter on the development of narrative as a viable pictorial mode. His narratives involve the fictionalized reconstruction of events associated with "our home life, which includes the care of a multiple handicapped child." While not so interested in documenting the day to day activities of existence, he focuses on allowing those activities to shape the aesthetic and formal decision-making regarding his painting. He says, "the exigencies of care-giving and judicious acts of triage (in caring for his child)," tend to inform his thinking. He finds himself "desiring to make works that contain concentrated essences of our histories and to carry these heraldries into the next century."

He sees painting as a reflection of the rigorous struggle for realization of one's own imagination.

"We live in a self-defining arena of action and consequence, where daily resuscitations bring us close to the awareness of human fragility and yet make plain the willful determination of our species."

Painting

ALIA E. EL-BERMANI

A recent graduate of the Art Institute of Southern California, Alia finds herself "solving the sometimes difficult puzzle of being an underexposed painter." She questions, as do other painters, how she can afford the time to paint and to also pay the rent. It is a balance between reality and passion; she works part-time to pay her expenses, but devotes most of her time to painting. She looks at this time as the "spring of career" where everything is blossoming and the future is all before her. She currently has exhibits on the West Coast, her work is included in selected collections on both coasts, and she has won several awards for her talent.

Painting for Alia is an internal, unconscious place, where her instincts out-weigh her intellect; a place where her thoughts and images mingle freely. She sees this as a process—sometimes unsuccessful—but believes that through this process she does her best work. She finds inspiration for her paintings in the human figure. Her classical figurative training has given her the useful tools to develop a "painterly, figuratively style." She prefers to paint large works to represent the human figure.

Alia found her four years at the Art Institute of Southern California invaluable. Through this educational experience she was able to refine her skills and to gain confidence in her work. She knew what she wanted to learn in school—and that was to learn discipline—and she also took classes in how to prepare for work in her field—"the do's and don'ts" of launching your career. Most important to Alia was that school provided her with a "warm, comfortable atmosphere" to develop herself as an artist.

As a student she remembers her work evoked the psychological tension she felt around her and she would focus this tension on her subjects as they sat for her painting. Then a teacher told her, "if we paint beautiful things, people must try to be beautiful." This moved Alia to change her perspective and she now focuses on the beauty she sees around her and the beauty in her subjects.

TOP
Portrait of a Friend, 1999
BELOW
Self Portrait, 1999
ARTIST PHOTO
Nancy Villere

"I try not to dictate the definitions of my paintings. Paintings exist differently for every viewer. We all have our own thoughts and experiences to define what we see. My one hope would be that through paintings, viewers can enter that internal, visceral space and enjoy it with themselves."

Painting

KIPP McINTYRE

"This creative process is never ending. Each of us strives for the most authentic expression of self that we are able to muster. Within us all is a unique identity that by nature strives to interact with other identities, thereby creating a new unique relationship that moments before might not have existed."

TOP
The Crossing, 1998

ABOVE
View from the Guesthouse,
from the **Falling Water**
series, 1999

RIGHT
Three Figures, (Monotype)
from the **Cylinder Seal**
series, 1999

Kipp graduated from the Atlanta College of Art in 1999, having taken a peripatetic route to that occasion. Kipp says he took longer to graduate then most students because he explored so many facets of the art world along the way. He actually started at the College in the early 1980s. While enrolled there, he went to Baltimore's Maryland Institute on a student mobility program for a year, met an industrial model-maker, and worked with him for two years.

Then he returned to the Atlanta area, worked for a few years as a studio assistant for one of his former professors, then moved to a local gallery for another few years, and finally went to the museum at Emory University as a preparator and an exhibition installer. A couple years ago, he returned to Atlanta College of Art to receive his BFA degree.

McIntyre says his education gave him the tools to develop his own way of doing things. It was an environment where ideas could be freely exchanged and discussed, and he could be challenged to do his very best. At the commencement ceremony he was presented with the College's Board of Director's Award. But even before that honor, he was exhibiting on a regular basis around Atlanta to favorable reviews.

He now teaches a class in the College's Community Education program on drawing techniques. On a grander scale, he founded the McIntyre Academy of American Art in Decatur, Georgia, only a few months ago so he could widen his impact as a teacher. He describes his daily activity as making his own art and helping others to make their art. Kipp encourages his students "to stay in touch with what's happening in the art world," while always remembering the value of learning about the past. Most of all, he says, "don't be afraid."

Photography

WILLIAM WEGMAN

William Wegman's photographs are whimsical, provocative and haunting. This work, as well as his drawings, paintings and videos, have been the subjects of many major museum exhibitions throughout the world. He has also reached audiences through his work on Sesame Street and a series of other educational children's books on fables, shapes, colors, numbers and the alphabet. He graduated from Massachusetts College of Art (MassArt) in 1965, and currently resides in New York with his family.

Known best for the photographs of his dogs (Weimaraners), there have been times when William resented being known as "the guy with the dogs." However, he now views it as a calling, one that is constantly both challenging and pleasurable. He realizes that a dog's life span is short compared to humans and he feels the need

TOP
Roller Rover, 1987

ABOVE
Blessing of Batty, 1997

to be there to capture the precious moments he shares with his canine friends. He says, "dogs don't try to give you a better angle. It's just so completely amazing that they can be become part of this process, and look right into the lens of the camera." When asked about his other works, he says that people are always surprised to find out that he has made, and continues to make things other than dog pictures.

He has a great fondness for his alma mater, MassArt. The school has one of only five 20" x 24" Polaroid camera in the country and he often returns to the college to create one-of-a-kind photographs with his famous dogs. He tells of coming from a not particularly "fancy" background and choosing MassArt because it was affordable. His childhood memories are that he "never was quite a part of things," but that changed when he went to art school. It was in college where he found out about religion, philosophy, music and "the other deep things in life." His education provided him with a venue to explore new and exciting things, and a chance to create with a new sense of internal meaning.

"After stealing into the modernist academy, busting up minimalism, abolishing conceptualism, scattering people in all different directions, I was allowed to do anything I wanted. Art movements get briefer every month. Styles come and go. So do mine."

Photography

NAN GOLDIN

It is hard to know about contemporary photography and not know Nan Goldin. Born in 1953 in Washington, DC, Nan Goldin has been photographing friends, acquaintances, and herself for over 30 years. On the occasion of her 1996 retrospective at the Whitney Museum of American Art in New York, the museum said her "raw and intimate work has become the signature of the sexual and cultural urban underground of the past two decades."

Nan is a 1977 graduate of the School of the Museum of Fine Arts in Boston. Since then she has had solo exhibitions of her work in all corners of the world, including Paris, Berlin, London, San Francisco, and New York. She has also won many awards along the way, including a National Endowment for the Arts Fellowship, a Louis Comfort Tiffany Foundation Award, and the Mother Jones Documentary Photography Award. And in addition to her photography, she has written and directed a BBC film and published several books of her own work.

Her photographs are unapologetic; she has photographed everything from the underground gay world, to drug use, abuse and rehabilitation, to destructive relationships, to the onslaught and devastation of the AIDS epidemic. It has been said that she "brings a rare sense of heart and humility to the fringe underworld" that she has documented since the 1970s.

The curator of the Whitney retrospective said Goldin photographs "from a position of unflinching emotional attachment to her subjects. Pulsing through all her work is a directness, a brutal honesty." Goldin refers to her work as "the diary I let people read....These pictures come out of relationships, not observation."

TOP
David with Joey at Edelweiss, 1991

ABOVE
C Putting on her Makeup at Second Tip, 1992

RIGHT
Queen Swallowing Fire, 1992

ARTIST PORTRAIT
Self Portrait on the Train, 1992

"My work is about what it's about, in the Buddhist sense. It's not about Anything else. I'm not referencing anything. I'm not referencing art history. I'm not referring to anything but life."

Printmaking

RALPH WOEHRMAN

Ralph Woehrman is a graduate of the Cleveland Institute of Art and is also currently the Chairman of its Drawing and Printmaking Department. As a young artist he saw printmaking as an ideal vehicle to create multiple images that commented on the social and political issues of the 1960s and 1970s.

He was convinced that his visual creations would have impact on society and assist in correcting what he saw as "critical problems of the day." Ralph's work has indeed made an impact, and he has been fortunate to exhibit his work throughout the country and to have his work collected by museums, colleges, universities, and private collectors.

Ralph's work relies on naturalistic images in mixed mediums, presented in very large scale. He now also does public works and mural commissions of sports narratives and American hero narratives. Collectors and commissioners of his work include such notable names as The Cleveland Indians, Dick Jacobs and Jacobs Field, the Fox Sports Network, Ralph Lauren, and Eddie DeBartolo, Jr.

TOP
Butterfly #4, 1999

ABOVE
Fox Sports Network, 1999

BELOW LEFT
Expatriated Bird #2, 1990

"The printmaking disciplines have evolved through centuries of traditional conventions. Today's printmaking students are witnessing the beginning of a technological revolution. New technologies allow students to expedite ideas with immediacy and refinement; ideas that possess complete archival resolution. Now, students have the opportunity to become technologically innovative and compatible with the reality of the world outside art school."

Ralph looks back on his art education as ideal and thorough. It completely prepared him for the real world. His career as an artist/teacher has thus far been very rewarding providing him with "much inward gratification." What he learned in school (and what he continues to learn today) showed him his creative potential, which he feels is being continually challenged. Today, teaching is a way to remain artistically vital and to reaffirm his commitment to art.

Sculpture

MICHAEL CURRY

TOP
**Puppets
for Disney, Inc.**

ABOVE
**Times Square 2000
Celebration**

ARTIST PHOTO
Rebekah Johnson

A graduate of Pacific Northwest College of Art (PNCA), Michael Curry has collaborated with Julie Taymor on the PBS/American Playhouse film "Fool's Fire," the opera "Oedipus Rex" conducted by Seiji Ozawa at the Salto Kinen Festival in Japan, and the opera "Die Zauberflote" at the Maggio Musicale in Florence, Italy. On Broadway, he has worked on numerous shows including "Crazy for You" and "Kiss of the Spider Woman." Among Michael's most noteworthy contributions was as co-designer with Julie Taymor on the 1997 Tony award-winning Broadway production of the "Lion King."

Michael owns and operates Michael Curry Design and Sculptural Engineering in St. Helena, Oregon which produces large, live-performance-oriented puppets such as those seen at the 1996 Olympic Opening and Closing Ceremonies and the Disney Theme Parks. His most recent endeavor was providing the artistic direction for New York City's Time Square 2000 Millennium event. This 26-hour show was viewed by an estimated 4.5 billion people.

Being one of the world's leading puppet experts didn't come without a solid educational back-ground. Michael's time at PNCA taught him, "to verbalize and articulate my work. I learned how to control self-criticism and compensational vocabulary, and to organize the various disciplines into a cohesive whole. I was exposed to the value of a formal art history education."

"I've made the transition from studio/gallery artist to public artist, a choice based on the level of exposure I am now able to give the public. Instead of connecting with thousands, I am now communicating with millions. Therefore, communication is broader and my format provides a highly collaborative large group of artists."

CARLOS DORRIEN

"I lead a monastic life. There is a lot of isolation. I prefer to work that way. I don't like working with assistants, even on large, public projects. I believe in carving the work myself."

Carlos Dorrien was born in Argentina in 1948. His family moved to the United States when Carlos was 20 and settled in Rockport, Maine. Carlos, now a U.S. citizen also retains his Argentinean citizenship. Carlos has been carving stone since 1972, while studying with Reno Pisano at Monserrat College of Art. He exhibits his work in New England and South America and has won several major awards for his sculptures. Today, Carlos spends three days a week as a professor of art at Wellesley College. The balance of the week is spent at his home and studio in Vermont.

He had a passion for painting early on, but he always wanted to do sculpture particularly stone carving. Carlos is now most known for his large, abstract, sculpture commissions. Although his work alludes to humans, he doesn't consider himself a figurative sculptor. His figures grow organically out of stone. He comes upon the ideas for his floor pieces when he acquires stones which he feels wed themselves perfectly to what he wants to create. Oddly, he says, "the smaller scale sculpture and personal pieces I create have begun to suggest figurative elements. This surprises me."

In Carlos' sculpture, the splitting of the stone emphasizes his interest in line. His chiseled ruptures create multiple units from granite that was once an integral whole. It has been said that the "splits" share a kinship with the lines of drawing. The relationship his sculpture has to the floor are similar to the relationship a painting has to a frame.

TOP
ARCHIVAL STN/CRYTDS, 1989

ABOVE
The Wine Muses, detail, 1997

LEFT
Omphalos, 1995

ARTIST PHOTO
Rick Stewart

Textiles and Fibers

CHRISTINA ROBERTS

TOP
Batik Dots, 1995

BELOW
Floral Batik, 1995
Floral Batik, 1995
Slavonic Myth, 1993

Christina Roberts graduated from the Moore College of Art and Design in Philadelphia, Pennsylvania with a BFA in textiles. Since graduation, Christina has worked as the Project Manager and Master Printer for The Fabric Workshop and Museum, also in Philadelphia, a unique museum that actually creates the work which is then exhibited. In both 1997 and 1998, she was one of five international judges selected for the International Textile Competition in both South Korea and in Japan. Christina is also a freelance textile designer for clients like Liz Claiborne, Alexander Julian, Elizabeth Arden. She also lectures and teaches frequently around the world.

Christina sees the primary goal of her job at the helping visiting textile artists bring their ideas to life. Another facet of her job is as Director of the Museum's International Apprentice Program, where she invites and trains high school and college students who have a specific interest in fabric design. Apprentice students have come from Uganda, Kenya, Ghana, Japan, Korea, Finland and throughout all regions of Europe. The age of these international apprentices is usually much older and represent adults already working in the field of textiles.

One of Christina's current endeavors is trying to figure out how to produce products that have been designed by a tribe living along the coast of Papua New Guinea. The Maisin Tribe are in need of figuring out ways of producing products to be able to afford the cost of medicine and other essentials all the while maintaining their traditions and lifestyle.

In college she received the academic and creative foundation that allowed her to then experiment and explore new ideas. While there, she was encouraged to work as an intern at the Fabric Workshop and Museum.

"As textile technology expands across the United States, Europe and parts of Asia, hand woven and printed fabrics are becoming a lost art. Although hand textile production is a very old tradition that still exists in many parts of the world, it is part of a culture that needs to be saved."

Transportation Design

"I believe people purchase products for emotional reasons, not rational ones. The moment they reach into their pocket and pull out their wallet, it's an emotional decision; it's about the ability of the product to meet their aspirations. Automotive design is a form of communication. We're trying to design an experience."

J MAYS

look of every car the company produces—he may well be the most influential car designer on the planet."

Mays says that he looked at several art schools and had no idea that there was such a thing as automotive design. When he found this program at Art Center he couldn't believe that he could learn a craft and actually, "get paid to draw pictures of cars—it seemed too good to be true." His education was invaluable as evidenced by his enormous success both in Europe and now in the United States. Mays knew Art Center drew talented automotive design students. His experience there focused his attention; he found a curriculum that demanded his full concentration.

TOP
Thunderbird Concept,
Ford Motor Co.

ABOVE
New VW Beetle,
Volkswagen AG.

ARTIST PHOTO
Ford Motor Co.

J Mays was born in 1954 in Pauls Valley, Oklahoma, attended University of Oklahoma for a few years, and graduated from Art Center College of Design in 1980. Mays went right to work for Audi, in Germany, and is credited with the design of the Audi 80. In 1983, he moved to BMW in Munich to work on exterior design for the BMW 5 and 8 series. He then returned to Audi in 1984 as a senior designer. He was responsible for developing full-scale model proposals for the Audi 100, Volkswagen Golf, Volkswagen Polo and Audi Cabrio, and he also designed the Audi AVUS Quattro concept car.

After a decade in Germany, Mays came back to the U.S. in 1990 to be the chief designer in the new Volkswagen-Audi Design Center in Southern California. It was here that he and Freeman Thomas designed the Concept 1, the precursor of the widely acclaimed "New VW Beetle." Recently, Mays became design director for Ford Motor Company, where he supervises 900 designers world-wide and will oversee the launch of the 2001 Thunderbird. As the *New Yorker* said in a recent profile, "Given that Ford just bought Volvo, and owns Jaguar, Mazda, and Aston Martin, as well as the Ford, Mercury, and Lincoln nameplates—and that Mays is responsible for the

JAY SHUSTER

"In this day of saturated markets and hyper-pop culture, it is a rare opportunity for a person to conceive and realize their own dreams and convey them onto a film. Film design empowers the individual to imagine beyond anything humankind has ever known."

Born in Pontiac, Michigan, Jay Shuster credits his father, an industrial engineer for General Motors, for his interest in design and his mother for teaching him how to write. He was inspired by Ralph McQuarrie and Joe Johnston, designers of the first Star Wars trilogy, and automotive illustrator Ken Dallison. A graduate of Detroit's Center for Creative Studies (CCS), Jay moved to San Francisco in 1994. He worked in various multimedia and video game production companies before landing his current job as Concept Designer at Lucasfilm. Last year he finished working on "Star Wars: Episode I – The Phantom Menace" (he did much of the work on the Podracer) and has just started work on the upcoming "Star Wars: Episode 2" film.

He defines his job as fulfilling the director's vision through the "conception and design of costumes, architecture or any physical asset that aids in telling the story." He views the motion picture industry as fiercely independent and comprised of super hard working individuals who don't pursue set agendas or who need organizational structure to achieve success. He believes it is the drive to fulfill one's own passion and vision which governs the industry.

At CCS, although he majored in transportation and industrial design, Jay was able to "twist" course objectives to meet his interests in graphic design, storyboard art, and film-related concepts. In general, he believes that to be a Concept Designer, you need a design program that will "enhance the momentum that already propels you toward your pre-established goal." Designers need to be able to clearly illustrate ideas on paper, and build both rough and finished concept models using a vast array of materials. He also believes that through his educational process he was taught the importance of having an intrinsic knowledge of design culture.

63

RIGHT
Concept drawing of Anakin Skywalker's podracer, Star Wars: Episode I – The Phantom Menace. *Photo courtesy of Lucasfilm Ltd.*

ARTIST PHOTO
Susan Smith

Other Careers

Many art and design students major in one subject in college and stick with that specialty for years and years. Others might migrate to related visual arts areas as their lives progress. Still others, however, go further afield into areas that are tangential to, or even distinct from, the visual arts.

Arne Glimcher, for example, graduated from the Massachusetts College of Art in 1960 and went to do graduate study at Boston University. At the same time, he became interested in exhibiting the work of emerging artists of the 1960s and so started Pace Gallery in Boston. The Gallery moved to New York City in 1963 and soon was showing major artists of the time, including Louise Nevelson, Jim Dine, and Lucas Samaras. In 1993, Arne merged Pace Gallery with Wildenstein & Co., to form the largest art gallery in the world, dealing in Pablo Picassos, Mark Rothkos, and Henry Moores. And for more than a decade, Glimcher has also been a movie producer and director. His credits include "The Mambo Kings", "Gorillas in the Mist", and "Just Cause" for Warner Brothers.

David Sedaris graduated from the School of the Art Institute of Chicago in 1987, the third college he attended in an attempt to finally earn a bachelor's degree. In addition to his visual art abilities, however, he harbored a long-standing interest in writing. His sister says "He has written religiously since he was a teenager, but he'll never call himself a writer." Well, whatever David may think, he is certainly a writer now, having published a number of books ("Barrel Fever" and "Naked"), become a commentator on NPR's "Morning Edition," and won an Obie Award for his play "One Woman Shoe." After college he supported himself with some part-time teaching, as well as with jobs as a maid and a Christmas elf at Macy's. But no longer— his fourth book will come out in a couple months, and he is now a regular on NPR and in the pages of "The New Yorker" and "Esquire".

Art, Design and Education Resources

There is a vast array of organizations offering information about art and design and the educational process—so many in fact that a whole book could be filled just with this material. So with an eye toward efficiency, we have attempted to compile in this chapter some key organizations that present information you might want to access early in your educational endeavors. You are encouraged to contact these resources directly.

Rigo ØØ
Photo by Diego Diaz

Photo by Todd Hido

departments and art colleges. NASAD publishes a directory of accredited programs each year, and makes other helpful information available to prospective students and their parents and teachers.

ACCREDITATION

Accreditation is the process of assessing colleges to determine if they meet certain established minimum standards, whether specific to art and design fields or applicable to all fields of higher education. To achieve accreditation, colleges prepare thorough "self-studies" and are then reviewed for several days by a visiting team of experienced evaluators. Once initially accredited, colleges are subject to regular, periodic reviews. While accreditation is voluntary in the United States, it is nearly universal, and it is required if colleges wish to participate in federal financial aid programs. Students may want to check a college's catalog for information about its accreditation. Attending an unaccredited college might be risky.

There are six regional accrediting agencies across the country; each covers a specific geographic section (such as New England or the Western states). These agencies review all colleges offering bachelor or higher degrees and apply general academic standards to all institutions seeking accreditation. With very few exceptions, most art and design colleges have this form of academic accreditation. There are also specialized accrediting bodies which focus on specific programs and degrees; some of the relevant ones are described here.

Art and Design

National Association of Schools of Art & Design (NASAD)

11250 Roger Bacon Drive, #21
Reston, VA 20190
1-703-437-0700
www.arts-accredit.org

NASAD is the recognized accrediting body in the United States for all art and design programs on the college level. It currently accredits over 219 art

Architecture

National Architectural Accrediting Board (NAAB)

1735 New York Avenue, NW
Washington, DC 20006
1-202-783-2007
www.naab.org

Although this book does not specifically address architecture programs, many art and design colleges offer this major as well, and architectural design processes are quite similar to many forms of design discussed earlier in this book. To obtain a license to practice architecture anywhere in the United States, one must have graduated from an accredited architecture program with a Bachelor of Architecture, a Master of Architecture, or similar degree. The organization which administers the national architectural licensing exams is located in the same building as NAAB, and can be reached through the NAAB Web site.

Interior Design

Foundation for Interior Design Education Research (FIDER)

60 Monroe Center, NW, #300
Grand Rapids, MI 49503
1-616-458-0400
www.fider.org

In addition to the specialized accrediting body (NASAD) covering all art and design programs, there is an even more focused accrediting agency covering just Interior Design. It too has publications as well as useful information on its Web site.

PROFESSIONAL ASSOCIATIONS

There are many associations in art, design, and education. Their members are mainly practicing professionals in their respective fields, but student chapters on college campuses are often included as well. These groups hold annual conferences and usually have publications that can help guide students through the college and career selection process.

Architecture

Association of Collegiate Schools of Architecture (ACSA)

1735 New York Avenue, NW
Washington, DC 20006
1-202-785-2324
www.acsa-arch.org

ACSA is the professional association for all college-level architecture programs. It publishes an excellent guide to the field of architecture, which gives considerable background information and a full profile of each accredited architecture program in the United States and Canada.

American Institute of Architects (AIA)

1735 New York Avenue, NW
Washington, DC 20006
1-202-626-7300
www.aiaonline.org

AIA is the professional association for practicing architects in the United States. Some of AIA's activities are oriented toward prospective students and its Web site is worth a visit to gain a better understanding of issues in this field.

Art Education

National Art Education Association (NAEA)

1916 Association Drive
Reston, VA 20191
1-703-860-8000
www.naea.org

NAEA represents K-12 art teachers throughout the United States and undertakes a variety of activities in their support. Students interested in becoming elementary and secondary school art teachers will find helpful information here.

College Art Association (CAA)

275 Seventh Avenue
New York, NY 10001
1-212-691-1051
www.collegeart.org

CAA is the professional association for college-level art and art history teachers. It publishes an excellent guide to MFA programs in the visual arts in the United States. Its annual convention in February is a significant venue for college art students seeking college teaching positions.

Crafts

American Craft Council (ACC)

72 Spring Street
New York, NY 10012
1-212-274-0630

ACC represents all manner of crafts and crafts practitioners. It is affiliated with NASAD for matters of accreditation and academic standards.

Graphic Design

American Institute of Graphic Artists (AIGA)

164 Fifth Avenue
New York, NY 10010
1-212-807-1990
www.aiga.org

AIGA is the best-known association of professional graphic and communication designers in North America. It is also affiliated with NASAD in matters of accreditation and academic standards and has a number of publications of interest to students.

Illustration

Society of Illustrators

128 East 63rd Street
New York, NY 10021
1-212-838-2560

The largest association for commercial illustrators in the United States, the Society of Illustrators operates an annual contest and other programs for students.

Industrial Design

Industrial Designers Society of America (IDSA)

1142 Walker Road
Great Falls, VA 22066
1-703-759-0100
www.idsa.org

Industrial and product designers are represented by IDSA, which is also affiliated with NASAD. IDSA publishes a guide to industrial design and has other programs of interest to students.

WEB SITES AND OTHER PUBLICATIONS

Admissions

Online admissions information, college searching, and applications are exploding, as more and more students have access to computers. Frankly, there is a very large number of sites in this area, with enough new ones starting every year that it is hard to keep up. All offer search and application systems of varying levels of sophistication. We will mention a few of the more well-established sites:

www.collegeboard.org

www.collegeview.com

www.embark.com

www.petersons.com

www.princetonreview.com

Unfortunately, you will find that art and design fields are a relatively small part of the overall college universe (representing less than four percent of all college enrollments), so conducting searches for very specialized subjects such as ceramics or animation might be disappointing at most of these sites. One shortcut to a more detailed list of schools by majors is to look at the chart of undergraduate majors located in this chapter. The NASAD Membership Directory (see "Accreditation", p.66) is also a good resource for searching for colleges by major fields of study as well. It lists 219 schools and college art departments.

Turning to print, there are a vast number of books on college admissions and financial aid—at larger book stores they fill several shelves. The College Board, Barrons, and Peterson's are well established companies, and their guidebooks are among the best generally available handbooks. Peterson's also publishes a very good, complete guidebook called "Professional Degree Programs in the Visual and Performing Arts". It describes all the art, design, music, and dance programs in the United States that are accredited by their respective specialized accrediting bodies. In art and design, this includes all NASAD-accredited schools and programs.

Financial Aid

As with admissions sites, there are many addresses on the Internet dealing with financial aid and scholarships. In our view, the most complete and helpful site is:

www.finaid.org

We recommend you "bookmark" this Web site and refer to it often. It has unbiased and authoritative information that can cut through the maze of confusing information about financial aid and guide you through the application process. We also advise you to avoid sites that guarantee to locate scholarships for you (no one can guarantee your eligibility), especially those that charge a fee to find you a scholarship or say they will do all the work for you. There is so much free information on the Internet that paying someone to do this for you is a poor use of your money.

Portfolio Days

The National Portfolio Day Association (NPDA), a group of NASAD-accredited colleges, operates a series of more than 30 Portfolio Days around the country. Many of the AICAD colleges listed in the following pages host these Portfolio Days on weekends during the fall and early winter. For complete information about NPDA and a list of Portfolio Day dates and cities, visit:

www.npda.org

You can also contact any of the host colleges for additional information. Portfolio Days are an excellent opportunity to see many college representatives at one time, to obtain either casual or formal reviews of your portfolio, and to gather information about financial aid and other aspects of the admissions process. We strongly support the Portfolio Day system.

In addition to these specialized Portfolio Days, there are many large college fairs around the country organized by the National Association of College Admissions Counselors (NACAC). NACAC also organizes a smaller series of college fairs devoted solely to the visual and performing arts. Both of these kinds of fairs take place throughout the fall and early winter. You can usually obtain information about them from your high school guidance office or by contacting NACAC directly (1-800-822-6285) or visiting its Web site:

www.nacac.com

Carlos Villa
Photo by Todd Hido

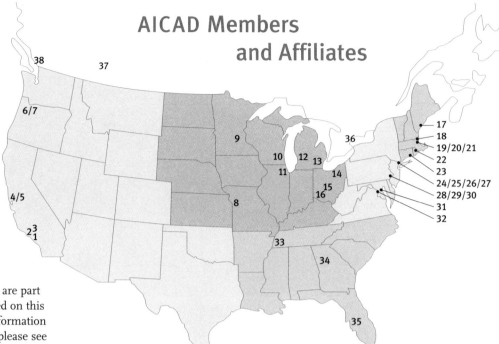

AICAD Members and Affiliates

The 38 colleges that are part of AICAD are located on this map. For further information about each college, please see the descriptive pages that follow. To request a catalog or application material, please contact the college(s) of your choice directly.

MEMBERS

west

1 Art Institute of Southern California . . p 79
Laguna Beach, California

2 Otis College of Art & Design . . . . p 101
Los Angeles, California

3 Art Center College of Design . . . . . . p 77
Pasadena, California

4 San Francisco Art Institute . . . . p 108
San Francisco, California

5 California College of Arts & Crafts . . . p 81
San Francisco & Oakland, California

6 Oregon College of Art & Craft . . . . . p 100
Portland, Oregon

7 Pacific Northwest College of Art . . . . p 102
Portland, Oregon

midwest

8 Kansas City Art Institute . . . . p 88
Kansas City, Missouri

**9 Minneapolis College
of Art & Design** . . . . p 96
Minneapolis, Minnesota

10 Milwaukee Institute of Art & Design . . p 95
Milwaukee, Wisconsin

**11 School of the Art Institute
of Chicago** . . . . p 109
Chicago, Illinois

12 Kendall College of Art & Design . . . . p 89
Grand Rapids, Michigan

13 Center for Creative Studies . . . . p 82
Detroit, Michigan

14 Cleveland Institute of Art . . . . p 83
Cleveland, Ohio

15 Columbus College of Art & Design . . . p 84
Columbus, Ohio

16 Art Academy of Cincinnati . . . . p 76
Cincinnati, Ohio

northeast

mid-atlantic

south

CANADIAN AFFILIATES

Hayami Arakawa
Photo by Todd Hido

Undergraduate Majors and Concentrations

This chart lists the undergraduate majors and areas of concentration available at the 38 colleges that are part of AICAD. Colleges use a wide variety of terms to describe their curricular offerings, some of which differ only slightly from each other. We have grouped some areas together under one phrase where appropriate—for example, Industrial Design/Product Design. However, a few areas are listed separately even though they are reasonably similar to another listing—for example, Graphic Design and Communication Design. This is done to reflect the colleges' own terminology and to recognize the breadth of certain fields.

We suggest reviewing the entire list carefully and checking all related areas so as to avoid overlooking a potentially suitable college.

According to NASAD's standards, at least 25 percent of the total course work towards the degree must be in a particular field of study for it to be called a major. Subjects accorded less than 25 percent are called areas of concentration or minors; often, these are subsets of a larger, related major. This list can be used as a preliminary guide, but there is no substitute for a thorough catalog examination.

● Major
○ Area of Concentration or Minor

#	College	Page	advertising design	animation | computer animation	architecture | architectural design	art | studio art	art direction	art education | design education	art history, theory, criticism	book arts | papermaking	cartooning | comic illustratio	ceramics, clay
1	Art Institute of Southern California	p 79	●			●		○				
2	Otis College of Art & Design	p 101		●		●						
3	Art Center College of Design	p 77	●									
4	San Francisco Art Institute	p 108										●
5	California College of Arts & Crafts	p 81			●							●
6	Oregon College of Art & Craft	p 100								○		○
7	Pacific Northwest College of Art	p 102										●
8	Kansas City Art Institute	p 88						●				●
9	Minneapolis College of Art & Design	p 96	●	●							●	●
10	Milwaukee Institute of Art & Design	p 95										●
11	School of the Art Institute of Chicago	p 109			●			●				●
12	Kendall College of Art & Design	p 89				●		●				
13	Center for Creative Studies	p 82		●		○						○
14	Cleveland Institute of Art	p 83										●
15	Columbus College of Art & Design	p 84	●	○								○
16	Art Academy of Cincinnati	p 76						●				
17	Maine College of Art	p 91						○		●		●
18	Montserrat College of Art	p 97			○			○				
19	Art Institute of Boston	p 78		○				○				
20	Massachusetts College of Art	p 93	●	●								●
21	School of the Museum of Fine Arts, Boston	p 110	●	●				○		●	●	●
22	Rhode Island School of Design	p 106	●		●							●
23	Lyme Academy of Fine Arts	p 90						○				
24	Pratt Institute	p 105	●	●	●	●	●	●				●
25	School of Visual Arts	p 111	●	●	●	●					●	
26	Parsons School of Design	p 103	○	●			○					●
27	Cooper Union, School of Art	p 85			●	○						
28	Moore College of Art & Design	p 98						●	○			
29	Pennsylvania Academy of the Fine Arts	p 104										
30	University of the Arts	p 112	●									○
31	Maryland Institute, College of Art	p 92		○			○	○		○		
32	Corcoran College of Art & Design	p 86				●				○		
33	Memphis College of Art	p 94	○	○		●						○
34	Atlanta College of Art	p 80	●	●		●						
35	Ringling School of Art & Design	p 107		●								
36	Ontario College of Art & Design	p 99	○									
37	Alberta College of Art & Design	p 75										●
38	Emily Carr Institute of Art & Design	p 87		●								○

© AICAD

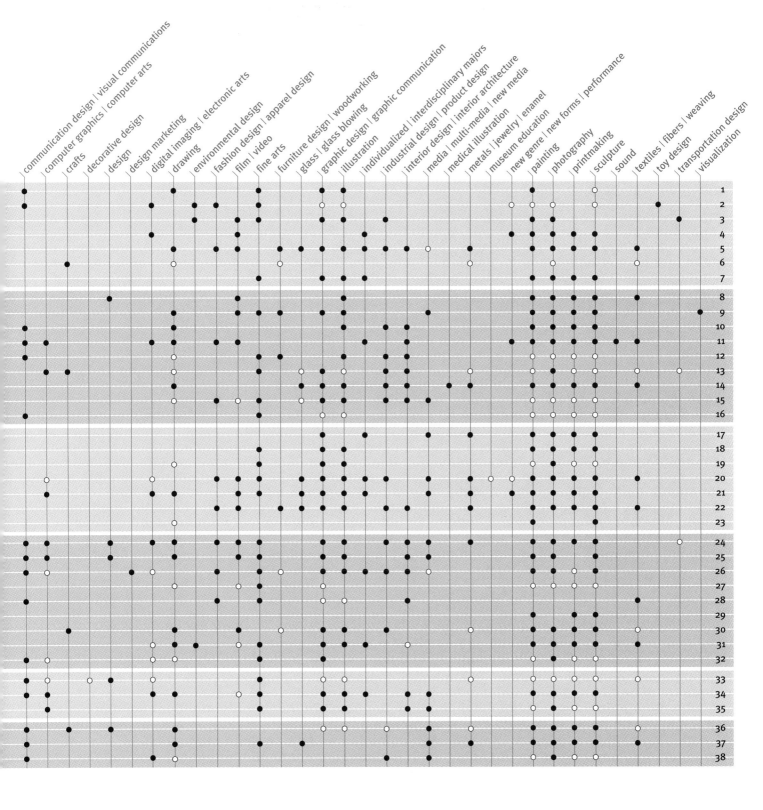

**Stephen Wirtz Gallery,
San Francisco**
Artwork by Todd Hido

AICAD College Descriptions

AICAD has 35 member colleges and 3 Canadian affiliates, all of which are described in the pages following. At the top of each page is contact information which may be used to ask questions, as well as to request catalogs, and admissions and financial aid applications.

The colleges described are degree-granting, NASAD-accredited (and in almost all cases, regionally accredited as well), specialized colleges of art and design. Unless otherwise noted, all BFA degrees are four years in length and all MFA degrees are two years in length.

The "FTE enrollment" shown for each school represents the number of full-time students plus the part-time students expressed as "full-time equivalents" (for instance, two students attending half-time equals one "full-time equivalent").

Many of these colleges are affiliated with nearby universities and thus are able to offer more extracurricular activities and support services than might be found at a typical small college. Almost all professional art colleges have "mobility" programs, whereby students may attend another art college for a semester, usually in their junior year.

Similarly, most art colleges afford students the opportunity to study abroad for a semester or for one year, or to arrange part-time jobs or internships while still enrolled. Many AICAD members also participate in a New York Studio Program, allowing students to spend a semester in New York City doing independent studio work or a professional internship. All of these special programs will be described in their catalogs, so again, we advise that you read them thoroughly. And as always, call the admissions office if you have any questions.

Alberta College of Art & Design

1407 14th Avenue, NW
Calgary, Alberta
T2N 4R3 Canada

1-403-284-7600 MAIN PHONE
1-800-251-8290 ADMISSIONS
1-403-284-7644 FAX

www.acad.ab.ca
admissions@acad.ab.ca

FTE ENROLLMENT 750
DEGREES OFFERED Diploma, BFA

Alberta College of Art and Design is a public college that offers four-year Diploma and BFA degree programs in the visual arts and design. The curriculum is wide-ranging, encompassing all aspects of studio practice in visual art and design, and liberal arts studies.

The College is located in Calgary, Alberta, Canada, nestled in the foothills of the Rocky Mountains, overlooking the Bow River and the downtown skyline, in a 245,000-square-foot building designed specifically as an art and design college. Studios are spacious and the classes are small. The College is home to two galleries—the public Illingworth Kerr Gallery and the student-run Marion Nicoll Gallery—as well as an outstanding collection of books, slides, and periodicals on contemporary and historical art in the Luke Lindoe Library. Other on-site facilities include an art supply bookstore and a cafeteria under the direction of the Student Association.

A connecting Light Rapid Transit station offers ACAD students easy, inexpensive access to the wider world of Calgary, including museums, galleries, theaters, the zoo, public libraries, and the University of Calgary.

ACAD students may participate in a variety of public service projects and practicum placements throughout the city. In addition, the College offers exchange programs that permit students to pursue a year of study at other institutions in Canada, the United States, Europe, Asia, and Australia.

Art Academy of Cincinnati

1125 Saint Gregory Street
Cincinnati, OH 45202
1-513-721-5205 MAIN PHONE
1-800-323-5692 ADMISSIONS
1-513-562-8778 FAX

www.artacademy.edu
admissions@artacademy.edu

FTE ENROLLMENT 210
DEGREES OFFERED
AS, BFA, MA

The Art Academy of Cincinnati, established over 130 years ago, was an integral part of the Cincinnati Art Museum for over a century. It recently became a fully independent college of art and design. The defining characteristics of the Art Academy are our small size, an emphasis on both fine arts and design, a range of courses from traditional life drawing to digital design, and close advising and mentoring of students by the full-time faculty and staff. With 200 full-time students, 15 full-time faculty, and a focused curriculum, the college draws serious and committed students. The faculty of professional artists, designers and scholars is committed to challenging students intellectually, conceptually and aesthetically. Students receive both consistent support and constant challenge—the goal is for students to internalize the creative and critical processes to arrive at a point after which guidance is no longer needed.

Beyond the training of artists and designers through four undergraduate degree programs, the Academy assists certified art teachers in a Master of Arts in Art Education program and each year provides 2,500 individuals with noncredit Community Education classes in the visual arts. Community Education classes range from those for young children to those for adults with leisure-time interest in art to professionals continuing their training. Through these programs and many community involvements, the Art Academy of Cincinnati serves as an extremely active small college, focused on its students and engaged in its community.

Art Center College of Design

www.artcenter.edu

1700 Lida Street
Pasadena, CA 91103-7197
1-626-396-2200 MAIN PHONE
1-626-396-2373 ADMISSIONS
1-626-795-0578 FAX

FTE ENROLLMENT 1440
DEGREES OFFERED
BFA, BS, MFA, MS, MA

Art Center offers a focused educational program that requires students to declare a major upon entry. Students commit to an intensive program that includes five major-specific studio courses each semester as well as a full program of liberal arts. Interdisciplinary work is encouraged, but students enter ready to focus on a specialization. For this reason, most students attend another college before applying to Art Center. Classes meet all year long and students have the option of accelerating their studies by enrolling for three semesters a year.

Art Center is located in Pasadena, within 20 minutes of Los Angeles, and is housed in an extraordinary contemporary facility overlooking the Rose Bowl. Facilities and technological resources are exceptional.

The college has a longstanding tradition of working closely with industry to assure that students are receiving the most relevant projects; many projects are sponsored by industry to take advantage of cutting-edge thinking that is the hallmark of the classroom experience.

The philosophy of the college is to encourage global and conceptual expression along with the development of strong communication and technical skills. Exchange programs are available with Occidental College and California Institute of Technology.

Art Institute of Boston

700 Beacon Street
Boston, MA 02215-2598
1-617-585-6600 MAIN PHONE
1-800-773-0494 ADMISSIONS
1-617-437-1226 FAX

FTE ENROLLMENT 490
DEGREES OFFERED
Diploma, BFA, Advanced
Professional Certificate

www.aiboston.edu
admissions@aiboston.edu

Founded in 1912, the Art Institute of Boston (AIB) is a professional college of visual arts offering programs and course work designed to prepare students for successful careers as illustrators, animators, graphic designers, Web designers, photographers, and exhibiting fine artists. AIB provides students with an intimate, challenging, and supportive environment that balances personal artistic expression with practical career goals.

After a rigorous first-year foundation, students choose a major that can include unique specializations, combined majors, or a wide variety of interdisciplinary courses and workshops. Studio classes are small and intimate—averaging 13 students per instructor—allowing for personal attention and an emphasis on the development of an individual style. As an integral part of our curriculum, students also explore the social, historical, and cultural influences that shape the world as well as individual interests that inform their imagination.

The majority of our students come directly from high school, with one-third transferring from other colleges or returning to college with some life experience. Our student body comes from thirty-three states and twenty-seven foreign countries, creating a global community of young artists with a stimulating variety of backgrounds and viewpoints.

Located in one of the country's leading educational and cultural centers, students at AIB benefit from the vast resources of Boston and our association with a larger institution (Lesley University), while learning within an intimate, supportive community of working professional artists. Students make professional connections through internships and freelance opportunities, giving them access to a network of career opportunities after graduation.

Art Institute of Southern California

2222 Laguna Canyon Road
Laguna Beach, CA 92651-1136
1-949-376-6000 MAIN PHONE
1-800-255-0762 ADMISSIONS
1-949-376-6009 FAX

www.aisc.edu
admissions@aisc.edu

FTE ENROLLMENT 240
DEGREES OFFERED
Certificate, BFA

The college was founded in the early 1960s and moved to its current location in 1977—a new campus designed to harmonize with its natural canyon setting. The Institute is one of only six fully accredited, independent, non-profit, art and design colleges in California, and the only one located south of Los Angeles. It offers a choice of four majors leading to the BFA degree: Drawing and Painting, Animation, Graphic Design, and Illustration. Students may also complete minors in each of those major subject areas as well as in Art History. All liberal arts requirements for the BFA are taught on campus.

The Art Institute's philosophy stresses the importance of skills as the center of artistic imagination, and its curriculum—in both studio and liberal arts—reinforces these values. The Art Institute's mission is to graduate intellectually and visually literate artists and designers, who are highly competent in both drawing and digital skills, capable of sustained effort in pursuit of their vision, and able to add immeasurably to our culture.

Artists have long been lured to the beauty and coastline of Laguna Beach, midway between Los Angeles and San Diego. The balmy climate and suffused sunlight, reminiscent of the Mediterranean, inspired the California Impressionist school of "plein air" painters. Now a city of 25,000, Laguna continues to project a village atmosphere—safe, friendly, and centered on the arts. The Laguna Art Museum, The Laguna Playhouse, summer art festivals, and the Art Institute draw thousands of art lovers to the community each year. Laguna's location, only 45 miles from Los Angeles' array of cultural and entertainment venues, enables residents to enjoy the best of all worlds.

Atlanta College of Art

1280 Peachtree Street NE
Atlanta, GA 30309
1-404-733-5001 MAIN PHONE
1-800-832-2104 ADMISSIONS
1-404-733-5201 FAX

FTE ENROLLMENT 400
DEGREES OFFERED
BFA

www.aca.edu
acainfo@woodruffcenter.edu

Founded in 1928, the Atlanta College of Art is the oldest college of art and design in the Southeast, and the only accredited four-year art college in the nation that shares its campus with a museum, a theater company and a symphony orchestra (the Woodruff Arts Center). This rich and diverse cultural environment stands in the heart of Atlanta, a city known for its booming economic growth and promise as well as for its celebration of history and tradition.

Atlanta College of Art students are immersed in a community of professionals who are dedicated to the development of thought, imagination, and skills. Working with faculty who not only teach but are practicing professionals, students are challenged to synthesize new information, ideas and technology toward the pursuit of creative excellence. The faculty to student ratio is less than 10:1. The Arts Center campus and the thriving city of Atlanta provide valuable professional opportunities for interns and graduates.

The College maintains three gallery spaces, exposing students to works by contemporary artists from around the world while also providing them a public forum for exhibition and discussion of their own works. The College also hosts visiting lecturers and artists-in-residence throughout the year.

Over 400 students from many diverse ethnic and cultural backgrounds converge on the Atlanta College of Art campus to create a community of divergent voices and viewpoints. While some of the students live in campus housing in midtown Atlanta, others choose to live in metropolitan Atlanta. Students major in thirteen different areas of study, with the largest number choosing Communication Design. Fifty percent study fine arts, and fifty percent study design or electronic arts disciplines. Last year, 2,300 area residents also took classes through the community education program.

California College of Arts & Crafts

111 Eighth Street
San Francisco, CA 94107
1-415-703-9500 MAIN PHONE
1-800-447-1ART (1278) ADMISSIONS
1-415-703-9539 FAX

FTE ENROLLMENT 1030
DEGREES OFFERED
BFA, BArch, MFA, MA

www.ccac-art.edu
enroll@ccac-art.edu

Founded in 1907 at the height of the Arts and Crafts movement, the California College of Arts and Crafts (CCAC) is dedicated to providing a rigorous visual arts program that maintains a healthy mix of theory and practice. Known for its interdisciplinary curriculum and the breadth of its programs, CCAC offers sixteen undergraduate degree programs through its schools of fine arts, design, and architectural studies. Four graduate programs are offered: the MFA Program in Design, the MFA Program in Fine Arts, the MA Program in Visual Criticism, and the MFA Program in Writing.

Located in the culturally rich and scenic San Francisco Bay Area, the College maintains two campuses—one in Oakland and one in San Francisco. The schools of architecture and design, as well as the graduate program and selected fine arts programs are based in a beautiful light-filled structure located in the heart of San Francisco's design district. The School of Fine Arts is based on the Oakland campus, which features a blend of Victorian and modern structures in a four-acre garden setting.

CCAC's faculty of practicing artists, designers, and scholars offers students a strong foundation in basic skills as well as an entrée to the professional arena. Students also benefit from a variety of internship, community service, and study abroad opportunities. Exposure to leading-edge local, national, and international culture is also an important part of the CCAC experience. The CCAC Institute offers a wide range of programs including exhibitions, lectures, artist residencies, symposia, and publications in the field of art, architecture, and design.

Center for Creative Studies

201 East Kirby
Detroit, MI 48202-4034
1-313-664-7400 MAIN PHONE
1-800-952-ARTS ADMISSIONS
1-313-872-2739 FAX

www.ccscad.edu
admissions@ccscad.edu

FTE ENROLLMENT 960
DEGREES OFFERED
BFA

CCS's superb faculty of accomplished professionals is deeply committed to developing students' technical skills, visual literacy, and analytical and conceptual ability. CCS's graduates are able not only to adapt to change but to lead it.

An education at the Center for Creative Studies College of Art and Design is about becoming a professional. A strong foundation, intensive studio majors, diverse liberal arts courses, and interdisciplinary opportunities combine to produce graduates who will shape the future of their fields.

CCS is a dynamic mix of traditional and high-tech arts. The College grants the Bachelor of Fine Arts degree in Animation and Digital Media, Communication Design (art direction, illustration, graphic design), Crafts (glass, fiber, ceramics, metals), Fine Arts (painting, sculpture, printmaking), Industrial Design (product design, transportation design), Interior Design, and Photography (applied, fine art, biomedical). Graduates go on to a variety of careers as leading auto designers, film industry animators, advertising art directors, photographers, fine artists, textile designers, and many others.

CCS's facilities already rank among the best in the country, with advanced computing studios, a foundry, hot glass studio, and excellent wood and metals shops. Its campus—in Detroit's Cultural Center next to the world-renowned Detroit Institute of Arts—is now in a major expansion. The new 100,000 square-foot Walter B. Ford II Building will open in fall 2000. It will be a fully digital building, with extensive computer labs and classrooms, an auditorium, and ample student workspace. A new campus quadrangle will give CCS an expanded sense of unity and community.

Cleveland Institute of Art

11141 East Boulevard
Cleveland, OH 44106-1710
1-216-421-7000 MAIN PHONE
1-800-223-4700 ADMISSIONS
1-216-421-7438 FAX

www.cia.edu
admiss@gate.cia.edu

FTE ENROLLMENT **510**
DEGREES OFFERED
BFA

The Cleveland Institute of Art is the only fully accredited professional art college in the country with a five-year degree program. The success of our graduates depends directly on the first two years spent in Foundation study. During these intensive years, students develop the essential skills needed for entrance to all fifteen majors.

Drawing, Painting, Design, Art History, and Literature make up the core curriculum of both Foundation years. A traditional Renaissance approach to drawing and painting from live models is emphasized. An understanding human anatomy and the ability to represent it two-dimensionally results in superior perceptual skills. Composition, color theory, and the organization of 2D and 3D space are the focus of Design classes. Art History begins with the Paleolithic era and continues chronologically through the late Twentieth and early Twenty-first Century. Written works contemporary to each era of Art History are studied in Literature, which also encompasses composition and critical analysis. Two computer courses are required and serve as an introduction to the use of software as a tool for art and design. Second-year students have an open studio elective each semester. Majors offer elective classes so that students will be able to make informed decisions about a major to pursue during the next three years.

Each of the majors at CIA is categorized into one of three disciplines—Fine Arts, Crafts, and Design. Interaction between these disciplines is critical to curriculum strength. Regardless of major, all students take courses outside of their discipline. Liberal arts electives also play an important role in a student's development as a professional artist. The course and credit requirements differ according to major, and there is opportunity to minor in four liberal arts areas, as well.

The culmination of the five-year program is the BFA thesis and review—required for graduation—during which candidates exhibit their work and receive formal critiques by fellow students and faculty. Most of the fifth year is spent independently preparing for this review, much the same way that one would prepare work for an agency or develop a body of work for a gallery show.

Columbus College of Art & Design

107 North Ninth Street
Columbus, OH 43215-1758
1-614-224-9101 MAIN PHONE
1-614-222-3261 ADMISSIONS
1-614-232-8344 FAX

FTE ENROLLMENT 1310
DEGREES OFFERED
BFA

www.ccad.edu
admissions@ccad.edu

Columbus College of Art and Design, founded in 1879, is one of the oldest and largest private art colleges in the United States. CCAD advances a distinct, challenging, and inclusive learning culture by uniquely blending its tradition and commitment to quality with its commitment to educating students in the fundamentals of art and the humanities.

CCAD offers majors in Fine Arts, Illustration, Interior Design, Industrial Design, Advertising and Graphic Design, Fashion Design, and Media Studies as well as minors in art history and art therapy. Specialized concentrations are offered in package design, photography,

animation, fashion illustration, and computer graphics. Integrated within all major programs is a full complement of liberal arts courses, an essential for the development of well-rounded visual artists.

More than 1,400 students from 40 states and 28 countries attend CCAD. Artworks by students, faculty, and alumni as well as impressive traveling exhibitions, are on display in six galleries and throughout the campus. Campus facilities include the Schottenstein Residence Hall, a student center, the Packard Library, with more than 43,000 volumes, a cutting-edge electronic arts center, extensive studio space, and the 400-seat Nationwide Auditorium, used by both CCAD and the Columbus community.

Located in the heart of Ohio's largest city, CCAD's 17-building campus is adjacent to the Columbus Museum of Art and a short walk from the Columbus Metropolitan Library, the Ohio Statehouse, theaters, and a multitude of cultural and historical landmarks.

Cooper Union, School of Art

30 Cooper Square
New York, NY 10003-7183
1-212-353-4200 MAIN PHONE
1-212-353-4120 ADMISSIONS
1-212-353-4345 FAX

FTE ENROLLMENT 890 overall,
250 in the School of Art
DEGREES OFFERED
Certificate, BFA, BS, BArch

www.cooper.edu
admin@cooper.edu

The Cooper Union, founded in 1859, is the only full-scholarship college in the United States dedicated exclusively to educating students for professions in art, architecture, and engineering. Its three schools are located in Greenwich Village, New York City. The immediate neighborhood is one of the city's centers of intellectual and creative life.

The School of Art offers a BFA program to 250 students, who also study in the city's great museums, visit studios and galleries, and work at a wide range of internships. Students are gifted, diverse, and highly self-motivated. The School's objective is to bring to its students an understanding of artistic activity outside the constraints of usefulness, fashion, applicability, and consumption. To realize this goal, the school offers a broad and rigorous curriculum based on the principle that creative development thrives most in an interdisciplinary environment.

Cooper Union does not require declared majors. Students develop through exploration of multiple fields and are educated not only in specific disciplines but also in the complex interrelation of all the visual vocabularies. Many students live in our newly constructed dormitory, and all sophomores, juniors, and seniors have their own individual studios.

Corcoran College of Art & Design

500 Seventeenth Street, NW
Washington, DC 20006-4804
1-202-639-1800   MAIN PHONE
1-888-CORCORAN   ADMISSIONS
1-202-639-1830   FAX

www.corcoran.edu
admofc@corcoran.org

FTE ENROLLMENT 320
DEGREES OFFERED
BFA

86

There is a long tradition of partnership between art schools and museums. Surrounded by great art and frequently by contemporary masters, a museum-school is charged with the excitement of direct contact with the world of art. The Corcoran College of Art and Design is special, for it remains one of America's very few examples of a "pure" museum-art school by maintaining its original relationship to one of Washington's greatest museums.

The Corcoran's main campus is in the heart of Washington, one block from the White House. A short walk brings one to the world famous Mall, ringed by museums, galleries, and the country's most distinguished monuments. The Corcoran's Georgetown campus features brightly lit studios and classrooms, an expanded papermaking and silk-screen facility, and three state-of-the-art computer graphics laboratories, which serve as headquarters for the new Corcoran Computer Graphics Institute.

The BFA degree is offered in Fine Arts, Graphic Design, and Photography. In the first year, students follow a unified and structured Foundation Program. In the second year, students select a major. Fine Arts majors may concentrate in ceramics, computer graphics, drawing, furniture design, painting, photography, printmaking or sculpture. Graphic Design majors may concentrate in 2D and 3D design or digital publication. Photography majors may concentrate in fine arts photography or photojournalism. Sophomore studio courses are designed as a bridge for the ongoing development of technical skills and increasing personal knowledge of artistic expression.

In the final two years, the focus shifts toward personal vision, individual initiative and professional development. Internships, individual projects, and electives hone each student's specific career goals. Studies culminate in formal exhibitions of senior projects in the Corcoran Museum of Art.

Emily Carr Institute of Art & Design

1399 Johnston Street
Vancouver, British Columbia
V6H 3R9 Canada
1-604-844-3800 MAIN PHONE
1-800-832-7788 ADMISSIONS
1-604-844-3089 FAX

FTE ENROLLMENT **990**
DEGREES OFFERED
BFA, BMA, BD

www.eciad.bc.ca
admissions@eciad.bc.ca

Established in 1925, Emily Carr Institute is a leading postsecondary school of art and design, offering bachelor's degrees and diplomas in visual arts, media arts, and design. Named for one of the foremost Canadian artists of the twentieth century, Emily Carr Institute has played a significant role in the lives of its graduates, many of whom have made outstanding contributions to visual culture around the world.

The Institute is located on Granville Island in the center of Vancouver, an exciting cosmopolitan city, and Canada's great western port on the Pacific coast. Granville Island is the site of an urban renewal project, an historic industrial site transformed into a complex of studios, galleries, theaters, shops, and public markets. Set in the midst of this thriving community, the Institute's modern facilities retain the distinctive corrugated steel and timber structure of the original industrial buildings while incorporating vaulted galleries, spacious sky-lit studios, and expansive technical workshops.

The Institute provides a studio-based learning environment that encourages the connections between ideas, information, knowledge, and communication. Students develop intellectual rigor, critical thinking, and a range of skills and values that prepare them for life and career-long learning. All majors begin with a common Foundation (first year) program and students enter their major in the second year. Programs in Animation, Integrated Media, Photography, and Design have limited enrollments and admission to these majors at the second-year level is competitive. The Institute also offers a full complement of critical studies courses in art, media and design history, humanities, social sciences, science, cultural studies and special topics. Students can opt for a four-year diploma program in some programs, in which a greater number of studio credits and fewer academic credits are required.

Kansas City Art Institute

4415 Warwick Boulevard
Kansas City, MO 64111-1874
1-816-472-4852 MAIN PHONE
1-800-522-5224 ADMISSIONS
1-816-802-3309 FAX

FTE ENROLLMENT 550
DEGREES OFFERED
BFA

www.kcai.edu
admiss@kcai.edu

Kansas City Art Institute is a four-year college of art and design with a long and rich history of preparing gifted students for professional careers in the visual arts. Over a century ago, when KCAI began, its founders were inspired by the same ideals that propel the burgeoning excellence of this institution today: to provide a nurturing, challenging educational environment for driven students of contemporary art and design in the areas of art history, ceramics, creative writing, design, film, illustration, painting, photography, printmaking, sculpture, and textiles.

KCAI is an intensely creative community. Professional studio artist-faculty work closely with students to guide their artistic and intellectual growth. Course work with full-time liberal arts faculty enhances the studio curriculum, assisting the development of creative problem-solving skills and broadening the field of knowledge so vital to the development of a serious personal aesthetic. KCAI students will find themselves considering the critical issues that face contemporary artists and designers, in a manner which reflects the integral role of the visual arts in contemporary life.

A vital addition to our educational environment is the new H&R Block Art Space of the Kansas City Art Institute. With this new art space, students will have the opportunity to learn firsthand from pivotal works of contemporary art. Through the many galleries and museums within walking distance of our campus, our students have immediate access to a wide range of established and emerging artists from across the globe.

The combination of elements which merge to form KCAI, results in a very special educational experience. KCAI is the place for serious study of contemporary art.

Kendall College of Art & Design

111 Division Avenue North
Grand Rapids, MI 49503-3194
1-616-451-2787 MAIN PHONE
1-800-676-2787 ADMISSIONS
1-616-451-9867 FAX

FTE ENROLLMENT 560
DEGREES OFFERED
BFA, BS

www.kcad.edu
packarda@kcad.edu

education. Kendall provides a personalized approach to education that not only helps students learn the principles of visual thinking but also provides the skills necessary to achieve career success.

Kendall College of Art and Design, founded in 1928, offers an education in art and design to a select group of students who are serious about refining their talent and who seek in-depth preparation for significant careers. The faculty consists of working artists, designers, and scholars dedicated to providing students with the necessary tools to explore and pursue their own creativity. Faculty members continually weigh changing methods and technology, striving to provide students with meaningful, real-world experiences while maintaining a solid and proven art and design

Kendall offers a BFA degree in Fine Arts (painting, drawing, printmaking, photography, woodworking as functional art), Furniture Design, Illustration, Industrial Design, Interior Design, and Visual Communications (graphic design, advertising, multi-media, and video). A BS degree is offered in Art History. The College's individual majors are based on a strong Foundation program that includes intense classical training while also allowing freedom and variety. A wide range of special lectures, exhibits, and seminars by noted artists and designers enhance the academic environment.

Lyme Academy of Fine Arts

84 Lyme Street
Old Lyme, CT 06371
1-860-434-5232 MAIN PHONE
1-860-434-5232 ext 122 ADMISSIONS
1-860-434-8725 FAX

www.lymeacademy.edu
admissions@lymeacademy.edu

FTE ENROLLMENT 80
DEGREES OFFERED
Certificate, BFA

The Lyme Academy is an independent, fine-arts-only college. Our mission is to provide the best possible education in drawing, painting, and sculpture through the study of the history, traditions, and principles of the fine arts and the liberal arts and sciences, thereby establishing a comprehensive foundation for the development of the artist.

The Academy's curriculum is based on a respect for classical values and reflects the same traditional forms of teaching which have produced master artists throughout the ages. The goal is to provide an educational foundation that will enable students to define their own work in diverse contexts through knowledge and experience, and with confidence and integrity.

Therefore the educational program at the Academy seeks to develop these qualities: craftsmanship and technical skill in the use of materials and methods; discipline, as intuition and creativity are subjected to judgment and revision; knowledge of the history of art, ideas, and human experience; critical thinking about ideas, events, intentions, and purposes; relentless pursuit of excellence; unique personal vision in each student; inspiration to fuel the intention and direction of the work; and respect for authenticity and aesthetic values.

Based on these principles, the Lyme Academy offers a strong, sequential program designed to develop intellect and imagination, intensity of observation, quality of execution, individual initiative and creativity, and depth of interpretation of ideas through artistic expression.

Ultimately, the Academy believes the fine arts are of unique importance as a defining and substantive element of society and life itself, and further, that educated artists are individuals who not only articulate their culture but give that culture shape and substance.

Maine College of Art

97 Spring Street
Portland, ME 04101-3987
1-207-775-3052 MAIN PHONE
1-800-936-4808 ADMISSIONS
1-207-772-5069 FAX

FTE ENROLLMENT **380**
DEGREES OFFERED
BFA, MFA

www.meca.edu
admissions@meca.edu

© Jennifer McDermott

Maine College of Art (MECA) is the only professionally accredited college of art and design in northern New England. Founded in 1882, MECA offers the Bachelor of Fine Arts (BFA) degree in eight studio disciplines, a minor in Art History, and a Masters of Fine Arts (MFA) degree in Studio Arts. Located in the heart of Maine's largest city, at the center of Portland's lively Arts District, MECA's spacious classrooms and individual major studios feature panoramic views of Casco Bay and historic Congress Street. MECA's 10:1 student to faculty ratio permits a high level of individual attention not found at larger institutions.

MECA's new Media Arts Center is equipped with the latest in audio, video, and digital art-making technology, enabling students to enter jobs that abound in digital art and design, both as students and as graduates. Courses in Illustration provide another practical avenue for students to pursue their art. A well-established Internship Program offers a variety of settings to gain hands-on experience in professional galleries, theaters, museums, design firms, and ad agencies, many located within walking distance of the College. An innovative Art In Service program offers paid service-learning internships with community agencies. A new joint program in Art Education with nearby University of New England provides focused training to students who wish to pursue careers as art teachers.

The city of Portland is rated as one of the top art destinations in the United States by "American Style" and "Outdoor" magazines, and has also been rated as one of the most livable cities in the United States.

Maryland Institute, College of Art

1300 Mount Royal Avenue
Baltimore, MD 21217-4191
1-410-664-9200 MAIN PHONE
1-410-225-2222 ADMISSIONS
1-410-225-2337 FAX

www.mica.edu
admissions@mica.edu

FTE ENROLLMENT 1300
DEGREES OFFERED
Certificate, Diploma, BFA,
BFA/MAT (5 years), MFA, MA, MAT

Maryland Institute, College of Art, founded in 1826, has long been recognized for its undergraduate and graduate programs and for its alumni, who have made names for themselves as some of the country's leading artists, designers, educators, and creative minds.

At the core of MICA's curriculum is a belief in the value of a firm grounding in the fine arts and liberal arts, the need for both technical and conceptual development, and the importance of the development of the individual artistic voice.

After completing the Foundation year, students choose a major (and often a minor), in which they gain the professional experience necessary to enter their career in art. At the same time, students are encouraged to cross disciplinary lines, to create linkages between the visual arts and the liberal arts, the fine arts and design, and technology and touch. Students can also expand their educational options by participating in one of 14 study-abroad programs, by gaining career experience in one of 900 internships, or by taking course work at one of Baltimore's other premiere colleges, such as Johns Hopkins University.

In addition to the major and minor areas of study listed in this brochure, MICA offers a unique five-year, dual degree BFA-MAT program, which combines an undergraduate degree focused on studio art with teaching certification at the master's level. For Fall 2000, MICA will inaugurate concentrations in video, digital multi-media, and animation. The Interior Architecture and Design department will be expanded and redesigned as a major in Environmental Design in Fall 2001. Minors are offered in liberal arts.

Housed in a beautiful and extensive campus of 16 buildings, students experience a rich residential living/learning/art making environment, with services that range from European style cafes to the Meyerhoff Center for Career Development.

Massachusetts College of Art

621 Huntington Avenue
Boston, MA 02115-5882
1-617-232-1555 MAIN PHONE
1-617-232-1555 ext 236, 238 ADMISSIONS
1-617-739-9744 FAX

www.massart.edu
admissions@massart.edu

FTE ENROLLMENT **1610**
DEGREES OFFERED
Certificate, BFA, MFA, MS

Massachusetts College of Art · 93

Established in 1873, Massachusetts College of Art (MassArt) was the first, and remains the only, four-year freestanding public art college in the United States. MassArt is recognized nationally for its innovative programs of visual arts education, paired with a strong general education in the liberal arts.

MassArt awards the BFA, MFA, and MS in Art Education degrees, as well as teaching certification and certificates in graphic and industrial design, and offers 17 areas of concentration. Continuing education classes fulfill the college's public purpose of providing access to the arts for the citizens of the Commonwealth. A major cultural force in Boston, MassArt offers public programs of innovative exhibitions, lectures, and events.

Approximately 1,600 graduate and undergraduate students are enrolled each year; another 900 take advantage of the Continuing Education program. The College draws motivated students from a large, diverse population, including many who transfer from other colleges. Approximately three-quarters of the students come from Massachusetts, and these students have the highest average SAT scores and high school GPAs among all the state's public colleges. The college also attracts talented students from 24 other states and 35 countries.

By developing students with broad visions, artistic maturity and specific expertise (including familiarity with the latest technologies), MassArt prepares them for a wide range of careers. For 126 years, MassArt graduates and distinguished faculty have helped to shape the worlds of art, education and business through their creative vision, leadership skills, and propensity for innovation.

MassArt is located on the Avenue of the Arts in the Fenway Cultural District, just steps away from Boston's premier cultural institutions, including the Museum of Fine Arts and the Isabella Stewart Gardner Museum.

Memphis College of Art

Overton Park, 1930 Poplar Avenue
Memphis, TN 38104-2764
1-901-272-5100 MAIN PHONE
1-800-727-1088 ADMISSIONS
1-901-272-5104 FAX

FTE ENROLLMENT 300
DEGREES OFFERED
BFA, MFA

www.mca.edu
info@mca.edu

Founded in 1936, the Memphis College of Art (MCA) is dedicated to excellence in art and design education. Conferring both the BFA and MFA degrees, MCA is the only dually accredited, independent art college between Kansas City and Atlanta and, notably, the only fully accredited art college south of Maryland and east of California to grant an MFA degree.

Situated in an award-winning building in historic Overton Park, MCA is small by choice and purpose. Its fine arts, design, and digital arts programs are both rigorous and individually created and guided. This is in keeping with the faculty's position that no single style or adherence should predominate as students are finding their own vision.

The College is distinguished among the nation's independent art colleges by its intimate scale, its remarkable faculty, its rich history, and its community support. MCA's student body is one of the most diverse among art colleges in the United States: 300 students who come from 30 states and 13 foreign countries. Approximately 80 percent of the student body receives financial assistance through scholarships, grants, loans, and work-study programs.

The College's faculty and local alumni include many of the most exciting and respected artists in the region, and other alumni can be found in distinguished design and fine arts positions throughout the world. MCA is accredited by the Southern Association of Colleges and Schools and the National Association of Schools of Art and Design.

Milwaukee Institute of Art & Design

273 East Erie Street
Milwaukee, WI 53202
1-414-276-7889 MAIN PHONE
1-888-749-MIAD ADMISSIONS
1-414-291-8077 FAX

FTE ENROLLMENT 580
DEGREES OFFERED
BFA

www.miad.edu
miadadm@miad.edu

The Milwaukee Institute of Art and Design (MIAD) is Wisconsin's only four-year, independent, professional art and design college. MIAD offers a BFA in: Drawing, Painting, Sculpture, Photography, and Printmaking, Communication Design, Illustration, Industrial Design, and Interior Architecture and Design. MIAD's studios and classrooms are in a newly-renovated, state-of-the-art, five-story, multi-windowed structure, with incredible light and wide-open studio spaces. The studio space per student is the largest in the country.

MIAD's curriculum is studio-centered, supplemented with a vital liberal studies component. The curricula for the majors reflect the latest thinking in professional needs, techniques, trends, and innovations. The ongoing emphasis is on problem solving. Committed to helping create artists who have both depth and breadth, our students find balance in the curriculum between a focus on their major interest, experimentation in related studios, and innovative cross-disciplinary study. Dialogue between departments and disciplines is constant.

MIAD has a relationship with nearby Marquette University, one of the nation's most respected universities. This collaboration combines the benefits of a small college of art and design with aspects of a large university, allowing MIAD students to have both academic and nonacademic extended opportunities. Students can take classes not offered at MIAD, such as dance, theater, and acting. They also have access to health services, psychological counseling, and the Recreation Center. Outreach programs are also plentiful at MIAD, including a unique blend of national and international exchange programs with other noted art and design colleges.

Minneapolis College of Art & Design

2501 Stevens Avenue South
Minneapolis, MN 55404-4347
1-800-874-6223 MAIN PHONE
1-800-874-6223 ext. 1 ADMISSIONS
1-612-874-3701 FAX

www.mcad.edu
admissions@mcad.edu

FTE ENROLLMENT 560
DEGREES OFFERED
BFA, BS, Postbaccalaureate
Certificate, MFA

Founded in 1886, the Minneapolis College of Art and Design (MCAD) is an independent, accredited institution offering a four-year curriculum integrating the liberal arts with 14 professional BFA degree majors in fine arts, media arts, and design; a four-year BS degree program in Visualization; a two-year MFA degree program in Visual Studies; and a one-year Postbaccalaureate Certificate program. MCAD also offers educational opportunities to the general public through its Continuing Studies, distance learning, and exhibition programs.

MCAD is dedicated to educating people as professional artists and designers who will become visionary leaders, creating the world in which we live. With a curriculum based on the belief that in order to become a professional artist, designer, or visualizer, one must study theory and skill, form and content, all MCAD programs center on the development of studio and professional skills, encouraging students to think conceptually, to formulate creative solutions and to make art. All MCAD programs challenge students to progress to the highest levels of artistic expression and intellectual investigation.

MCAD's seven-acre campus, one of the finest art college facilities in the country, shares a three-block area with the Children's Theater Company and the Minneapolis Institute of Arts in a residential neighborhood two miles south of downtown Minneapolis, a city known for its strong support of the arts.

Montserrat College of Art

23 Essex Street
Beverly, MA 01915
1-978-921-4242 MAIN PHONE
1-800-836-0487 ADMISSIONS
1-978-921-4241 FAX

FTE ENROLLMENT 370
DEGREES OFFERED
Diploma, BFA

www.monserrat.edu
admiss@monserrat.edu

Montserrat College of Art possesses a variety of advantages that distinguish it among the nation's colleges of art and design. With an enrollment of 380, the College is large enough to offer the wide array of courses that comprise a strong visual arts curriculum, yet small enough to provide the personal attention that is often difficult to find in larger schools. Our small classes encourage intensive, individualized instruction by a faculty of professional artists and designers and accomplished scholars.

Montserrat is a residential college; housing is nestled among the homes of historic downtown Beverly. Boston is 23 miles to the south and is easily accessible by car or commuter train. World-class museums, such as the Boston Museum of Fine Arts, galleries, libraries, shopping, sports, and a variety of entertainment options provide a stimulating intellectual, cultural and social environment in which to live and learn.

After the first year of Foundation studies, a student may choose to concentrate in fine arts, graphic design, illustration, painting and drawing, photography, printmaking, or sculpture and can also prepare for a career in art education. The Montserrat curriculum allows students to explore a wide range of studio electives to encourage the development of a unique artistic voice.

Students in Senior Seminar have the opportunity to delve independently into a significant, coherent body of work and to exhibit their seminar work throughout the spring. This revelatory experience helps students mature as artists and designers and, ultimately, make the transition into professional life.

Moore College of Art & Design

20th Street & The Parkway
Philadelphia, PA 19103-1179
1-215-568-4515 MAIN PHONE
1-800-523-2025 ADMISSIONS
1-215-568-8017 FAX

www.moore.edu
admiss@access.digex.net

FTE ENROLLMENT 430
DEGREES OFFERED
Certificate, BFA

Moore College of Art and Design is the first and only women's college for the visual arts in the nation. Located in Center City Philadelphia, the campus has two renowned galleries and is only a few minutes from world-class museums and cultural institutions, such as the Philadelphia Museum of Art and the Rodin Museum.

Moore students learn from a faculty of active scholars and practicing artists and designers. Bachelor of Fine Arts programs in fashion design, fine arts (two- or three-dimensional fine arts, general fine arts with art certification, studio art with art history emphasis), graphic design, illustration, interior design, photography and textile design prepare them to become confident and successful professionals, no matter where their career paths may lead.

Since 1848, Moore has remained true to the entrepreneurial vision of founder Sarah Worthington Peter, whose pioneering school of design for women bridged the world of education with the world of work, then primarily in the textile industry. Today, the BFA programs, as well as the Young Artist Workshop and Continuing Education programs, prepare students to meet the highest standards in the fields of art education, art history, and fine and design arts.

As a small, independent, single-sex college, Moore has become the college of choice for women with special gifts in the visual arts. Entering the new century, Moore remains committed to its historical tradition of educating women for successful careers in the visual arts while growing and adapting to the needs of future generations of artists and designers.

Ontario College of Art & Design

100 McCaul Street
Toronto, Ontario
M5T 1W1 Canada
1-416-977-6000 MAIN PHONE
1-416-977-6000 ext. 236 ADMISSIONS
1-416-977-0235 FAX

www.ocad.on.ca
jsage@ocad.on.ca

FTE ENROLLMENT **1700**
DEGREES OFFERED
Diploma

Located in the heart of Toronto's thriving cultural community, the Ontario College of Art and Design (OCAD) is a dynamic institution with an inspired heritage, an accomplished faculty and staff, and a lively, gifted student body. We are dedicated to providing students with high-quality, studio-based programs that prepare graduates for professional careers in visual and media arts and design.

OCAD offers four-year programs leading to an Associate of the Ontario College of Art & Design Diploma (AOCAD). The AOCAD is a well-recognized credential, identifying students who are prepared to thrive in a climate of rapid economic, cultural, and technological change.

Students entering their first year of study at the College begin in the Faculty of Foundation Studies. In the fall semester, the unified curriculum teaches visual basics in the "Principles" studio courses which focus on color, drawing, and two and three dimensional concepts. A liberal studies course complements the studio work by providing an overview of visual culture. In the winter semester, students choose to follow the Art or the Design stream and courses focus on preparing students for second year studies in the respective disciplines.

The Faculty of Art offers majors in Drawing and Painting, Integrated Media, Photography, Printmaking and Sculpture/Installation. Art students may focus on one discipline or combine across several areas.

The Faculty of Design offers opportunities for study in Communication and Design (Advertising, Illustration and Graphic Design, Environmental Design, Industrial Design) and Material Art and Design (Ceramics, Jewelry and Fiber).

Our Mission is to challenge each student to find a unique voice, to provide a vibrant and creative environment, to prepare graduates to excel as cultural contributors in Canada and beyond, and to champion the vital role of art and design in society.

8245 SW Barnes Road
Portland, OR 97225
1-503-297-5544 MAIN PHONE
1-800-390-0632 ADMISSIONS
1-503-297-9651 FAX

FTE ENROLLMENT 70
DEGREES OFFERED
Certificate, BFA

Oregon College of Art & Craft

www.ocac.edu
admissions@ocac.edu

OCAC's campus is located on 11 acres, three miles west of downtown Portland. There are separate and specially equipped studios for each department: book arts, ceramics, drawing, fiber, metals, photography, and wood. The central building houses the library, which includes the region's most extensive collection of books, slides, and periodicals of crafts, an exhibition gallery, a sales shop, and a cafe.

All studio faculty are exhibiting artists. In recent years, faculty members have helped organize the national conferences of their professional associations in Portland, including the Society of American Goldsmiths, Surface Design Association, and Handweavers Guild of America. There is an annual juried student exhibition in the Hoffman Gallery each spring and a group exhibition of thesis work at graduation. OCAC's Artist-in-Residence program brings both emerging and nationally known artists to Portland, providing them with the time, resources, and equipment to push their work in new directions while also interacting with students.

The Hoffman Gallery is a nationally recognized exhibition space that shows innovative work in fine arts and craft. Students gain exposure to professional gallery practices through participation in the annual Student Show, a faculty juried exhibition of the best student work, and their theses exhibitions.

The curriculum is structured to provide an appropriate balance of supervised and independent work. Innovations in programming include business practices and writing for the artist, concept seminars for exploring the content of work, and a professional practice class in developing, documenting, and presenting a line of work. In the final year of study, students prepare an original body of work for exhibition.

Otis College of Art & Design

9045 Lincoln Boulevard
Los Angeles, CA 90045-3550
1-310-665-6800 MAIN PHONE
1-800-527-6847 ADMISSIONS
1-310-665-6821 FAX

FTE ENROLLMENT 830
DEGREES OFFERED
Certificate, BFA, MFA

www.otisart.edu
otisart@otisart.edu

Otis College of Art and Design is located on the west side of Los Angeles on a 5-acre campus in the heart of Southern California's technical film, digital imaging, and toy design industries. The nearby communities of Venice and Santa Monica are home to many of Los Angeles' most important fine art studios and galleries. Otis is an "artist's art school," where the studios resemble artist lofts with high ceilings, open spaces, and exposed structural supports.

The College's commitment to exposing students to the professional art community includes programs ranging from internships to visiting artists. The curriculum which includes a very strong Foundation Program also includes opportunities to study abroad and experiences in local artist studios. The small class sizes and the diversity of the student body allow students to create a communal learning environment. Otis alumni include such historically recognized artists as Philip Guston, Robert Irwin, and John Baldesarri. The alumni also include academy award-winning costume designer Edith Head, as well as artists Paul Soldner, Billy Al Bengston, Kent Twitchell, Alison Saar, and Lita Albuquerque.

Over 800 students from 30 states and 20 countries are enrolled in BFA and MFA programs. They enjoy a talented and accessible faculty and the benefits of being located in close proximity to the Los Angeles art and design communities.

Pacific Northwest College of Art

1241 NW Johnson Street
Portland, OR 97209
1-503-226-4391 MAIN PHONE
1-800-818-PNCA ADMISSIONS
1-503-226-3587 FAX

FTE ENROLLMENT 280
DEGREES OFFERED
Certificate, BFA

www.pnca.edu
pncainfo@pnca.edu

© Eckert & Eckert

Edith Goodman Building is exceptional and has exceeded our highest hopes, the primary focal point of PNCA remains the community and the atmosphere. With dedicated faculty, helpful staff, and enthusiastic students, the PNCA community is small and fairly tight-knit, yet open.

We pride ourselves on superior facilities and a cutting edge environment, but it is the intangibles that make the College a special place. Our faculty members are all working artists, so in addition to the obvious instrumental benefits, there is direct sharing of "what it takes" to make it as an artist between teacher and student. Not many colleges have classes in which the instructor and students continue a discussion after class in a local cafe. PNCA attracts a certain kind of student, and we aim to present an environment that is conducive to their learning and growth.

In the heart of Portland's Pearl District is Pacific Northwest College of Art (PNCA), one of the oldest private art colleges on the West Coast. This longevity is a perfect fit with the school's philosophy of establishing and maintaining a traditional foundation in studio arts. Though our new location in the venerable

Parsons School of Design

66 Fifth Avenue
New York, NY 10011
1-212-229-8900 MAIN PHONE
1-800-252-0852 ADMISSIONS
1-212-229-8975 FAX

FTE ENROLLMENT 2520
DEGREES OFFERED
AAS, BFA, BBA, MFA, MArch, MA

www.parsons.edu
parsadm@newschool.edu

Parsons School of Design was founded in 1896 by American painter, William Merritt Chase. When Frank Alvah Parsons became the president, he responded to the Industrial Revolution by focusing the mission of the School on educating designers who would improve the quality, beauty, and usefulness of mass-produced goods. At the dawn of the twenty-first century, Parsons School of Design is now responding to the technology revolution and concurrent changes in the design industries, society, and culture. Located in Lower Manhattan in New York City, Parsons has close ties to both industry and the arts and a faculty of leading professionals.

A division of New School University since 1970, Parsons offers students the expertise of a professional art and design college as well as a broader university experience. Parsons provides extensive digital curricula and new, state-of-the-art technology facilities to support the revolution in multimedia, information design, and Web media. The Center for New Design is a project-based laboratory that enables faculty, students, and business to explore new technologies and methods and provide pathways to cutting edge curricula. The new Integrated Design Curriculum is a unique four-year program that blends studio and liberal arts within hybrid courses.

Parsons School of Design is a global college. Students come from all 50 states of the United States and from 60 countries. The School has international exchange programs in many parts of the world and affiliate schools in Paris, France; Kanazawa, Japan; Seoul, Korea; and the Dominican Republic.

Pennsylvania Academy of the Fine Arts

118 North Broad Street
Philadelphia, PA 19102-9791
1-215-972-7600 MAIN PHONE
1-215-972-7625 ADMISSIONS
1-215-569-0153 FAX

www.pafa.org
admissions@pafa.org

FTE ENROLLMENT **230**
DEGREES OFFERED
Certificate, BFA (with Univ. of
Pennsylvania), MFA

104

The Pennsylvania Academy's objective is to assist aspiring artists to reach their goals. To this end, the Academy offers a four-year Certificate program and a coordinated BFA program with the University of Pennsylvania, also located in Philadelphia, and a member of the Ivy League. The Academy also offers a two-year MFA program and a one-year Post-baccalaureate program. Each program has majors in painting and drawing, printmaking, and sculpture.

The Academy's curricula are all studio-based and require each participant to make an unequivocal commitment to the creative process. The instructional program fosters and protects the special empathy that must be struck between an instructor and student for the educational process to be meaningful.

© David Graham

The total student body at the Academy is approximately 300 undergraduate and graduate students who come from all walks of life, all age groups, and widely varying backgrounds. This creates a high-energy, enriching community, bound together by a passion for art and the creative act.

The Academy is located in the heart of Philadelphia, in close proximity to the many museums and historical and cultural landmarks that make up the thriving downtown community. New York City, Baltimore, and Washington, D.C. are all within two hours travel time.

Pratt Institute

100 Willoughby Avenue
Brooklyn, NY 11205
1-718-636-3600 MAIN PHONE
1-800-331-0834 ADMISSIONS
1-718-636-3670 FAX

FTE ENROLLMENT 3,560
DEGREES OFFERED
AOS, BFA, BID, BArch, MFA, MS,
MID, MPS

www.pratt.edu
admissions@pratt.edu

Pratt Institute is one of the largest undergraduate and graduate colleges of art, design, writing, and architecture in the United States. It is located on a 25-acre campus, with 27 buildings, including landmark Romanesque and Renaissance Revival structures, in Brooklyn's historic Clinton Hill section. Approximately 86 percent of first-year students live in one of Pratt's six residence halls. Pratt offers a traditional college experience with more than 35 student-run organizations, including fraternities, sororities, professional societies, clubs, and intramural sports teams participating in NCAA and ECAA men's and women's varsity sports.

Pratt's proximity to Manhattan, which offers a vast array of professional, cultural, and recreational opportunities, is a distinct advantage to students. Through Pratt's optional internship program, qualified students are offered challenging on-the-job experience in Manhattan's top galleries and design firms, giving them firsthand work exposure as well as credit toward their professional degree. This extension of the classroom into the professional world adds a practical dimension to their education which, combined with a strong liberal arts curriculum and rigorous professional education, prepares students to be leaders in their fields.

The fact that Pratt has one of the highest student retention rates in the country among colleges of its kind confirms the satisfaction students and their families report about the quality of the education they receive here.

Rhode Island School of Design

2 College Street
Providence, RI 02903-2791
1-401-454-6100 MAIN PHONE
1-800-364-7473 ADMISSIONS
1-401-454-6309 FAX

FTE ENROLLMENT 2120
DEGREES OFFERED
BFA, MFA, MID, MArch, MIntArch,
MLA, NA. MAT

www.risd.edu
admissions@risd.edu

© David O'Connor Photography

Students who come to RISD join an intense, creative, artists' community that has been internationally respected for its excellent education for more than 120 years. RISD's 2,000 students, coming from more than 50 nations around the world, find an extensive range of majors in the areas of architecture, design, and the fine arts. The college enjoys the advantages of a large full-time faculty, and has a student-faculty ratio of 12:1. Liberal arts form an important component of each student's study, and RISD invests notably in the quality of its academic course offerings. Fifteen percent of our students cross-register annually for courses at neighboring Brown University.

Our campus of 40 buildings is located on Providence's College Hill, which rises up to the city's historic East Side. RISD's 12,000 alumni have earned some of the most prominent positions of accomplishment and achievement in their respective fields and consistently win major competitions, prestigious awards, and recognition for their works in the arts, industry and education.

Ringling School of Art & Design

2700 North Tamiami Trail
Sarasota, FL 34234-5896
1-941-351-5100 MAIN PHONE
1-800-255-7695 ADMISSIONS
1-941-359-7517 FAX

FTE ENROLLMENT 880
DEGREES OFFERED
BFA

www.ringling.edu
admissions@ringling.edu

Ringling School of Art and Design explores the leading edge of the visual arts and design through its intensive four-year degree program. It confers the Bachelor of Fine Arts degree in Computer Animation, Fine Arts, Graphic and Interactive Communication, Illustration, Interior Design, Photography, and Digital Imaging. Interdisciplinary liberal arts courses are woven through the curriculum, grounded in the traditions of the studio and open to the possibilities of applied technology. All programs provide state-of-the-art technology and emphasize the development of a professional-quality portfolio in preparation for employment or graduate education. Ringling School is recognized as a leader in developing individuals to achieve their fullest potential as successful artists and designers and in preparing its students for careers.

Located on a residential campus on Florida's Gulf Coast, Ringling School provides exceptional facilities for learning and living. Admission is based on the student's portfolio, academic records, recommendations, and essay. We welcome applications from students with a serious commitment to the visual arts.

San Francisco Art Institute

800 Chestnut Street
San Francisco CA 94133
1-415-771-7020 MAIN PHONE
1-800-345-7324 ADMISSIONS
1-415-749-4592 FAX

FTE ENROLLMENT 570
DEGREES OFFERED
BFA, Post-Baccalaureate
Certificate, MFA

www.sfai.edu
admissions@sfai.edu

For more than 125 years, the San Francisco Art Institute has built a reputation as one of the premier fine arts colleges in the nation. The college has been the center of many of this country's most notable art movements and claims many of our nation's most important artists as faculty and alumni. At the vanguard of contemporary arts education, the Art Institute prepares its students for a rich life in the arts with an intensive studio environment and a vital liberal arts experience.

In the 1970s and 1980s, the San Francisco Art Institute was a leader in the development of conceptual art, new genres, film, and video, with a faculty that included George Kuchar, Ernie Gehr, Tony Labat, John Roloff, Karen Finley, David Ireland, Paul Kos, among many others.

In 1994 the Art Institute founded the Center for Digital Media, the nation's first state-of-the-art computer center dedicated exclusively to artistic explorations and the development of new media. The Center, along with other programs at the Art Institute, encourages art making that reflects a broad spectrum of forms, philosophies, and aesthetic approaches, and fosters critical thinking and creative development through an on-going and intensive critique process.

Today, more than 600 students study in the college's prestigious degree programs. Its reputation expands well beyond the United States borders, attracting students from Asia, South America, and Europe. Thousands more participate locally in public programs in the contemporary visual arts that include exhibitions, lectures, and extension education classes for adults and high school students. The San Francisco Art Institute strives to be a leader in promoting awareness of the relevance of the arts in contemporary culture.

© Todd Hido

School of the Art Institute of Chicago

37 South Wabash Avenue
Chicago, IL 60603-3103
1-312-899-5100 MAIN PHONE
1-800-232-7242 ADMISSIONS
1-312-899-1840 FAX

FTE ENROLLMENT 2040
DEGREES OFFERED
BFA, BIA, MFA, MA, MS

www.artic.edu
admiss@artic.edu

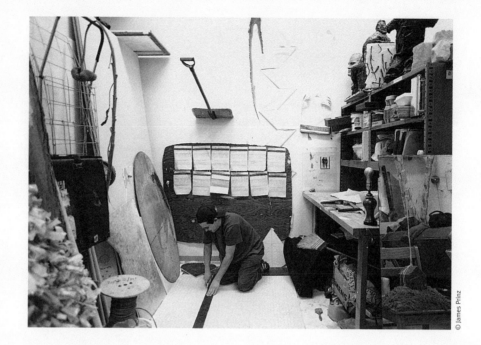

© James Prinz

For more than 134 years, the School of the Art Institute of Chicago (SAIC) has offered students a quality interdisciplinary education. The School attracts students who are motivated and disciplined artists who flourish in a self-directed studio environment. SAIC is an accredited college of the visual and related arts, offering degrees at the undergraduate and graduate levels. Its primary purpose is to foster the artistic and aesthetic maturation of its students in an environment that encourages the exploration and production of significant ideas and images while nurturing the development of individual excellence.

The School offers a broad and dynamic spectrum of course study. Majors are not required; instead students concentrate on single areas or a combination of areas that meet their individual interests. Areas of concentration include: art and technology; arts administration; art history, theory and criticism; art education and art therapy; fashion design; filmmaking; historic preservation and interior architecture; painting and drawing; performance; photography; printmaking; sculpture; sound; time arts (time-based media); video; visual communication; and writing. A comprehensive program in liberal arts emphasizes the pivotal role that humanities, mathematics, and the sciences play in artists' development. The School also serves as a national resource for issues related to the position and importance of the arts in society.

School of the Museum of Fine Arts, Boston

230 The Fenway
Boston, MA 02115-9975
1-617-369-3600 MAIN PHONE
1-800-643-6078 ADMISSIONS
1-617-424-6271 FAX

FTE ENROLLMENT 720
DEGREES OFFERED
Diploma, Certificate, and (with
Tufts University) BFA , BA/BFA ,
BS/BFA, MA , MFA

www.smfa.edu
admissions@smfa.edu

The Boston Museum School offers students the opportunity to design their own individualized course of study and to tailor a program that best suits their needs and goals. A division of the Museum of Fine Arts and affiliated with Tufts University, the Museum School offers a diverse curriculum with a full range of studio and academic resources. A large faculty of working artists and an intimate student-faculty ratio of 10:1 provide each student extensive opportunities for individual consultation and dialogue.

Similar to an artists' colony, the Museum School's focus is on creative investigation, risk-taking, and the exploration of individual vision. For artists working in this new century, individual vision may take many forms: private acts of object-making, performance, collaboration, electronic imaging, or computer networking.

In order to educate individuals who will become working artists of significance in local and global culture, the Museum School embraces a wide range of media and perspectives in the production of artwork. Similarly, the School makes available a number of different programs to accommodate the varied backgrounds and experiences of the individuals who attend the Museum School.

The School's extensive interdisciplinary studio curriculum is developed continually in order to incorporate new media and new approaches, concepts, and theories. A rapidly changing and culturally diverse art world is further introduced through the School's dynamic exhibition and visiting artists programs.

Students are free to work in a single medium or move across media, combining them according to their interests and inclinations. In this way, each student shapes a focus. Students may work in painting and video, in electronic imaging and stained glass, or in printmaking, film, and drawing—the combinations are endless, as are the results.

© Jim Fossett